THE 2001 ANTHRAX DECEPTION

THE 2001 ANTHRAX DECEPTION

THE CASE FOR A DOMESTIC CONSPIRACY

BY

GRAEME MACQUEEN

CLARITY PRESS, INC.

ISBN: 978-0-9860731-2-0
EBOOK: 978-0-9860731-3-7
In-house editor: Diana G. Collier
Cover: R. Jordan P. Santos

Library of Congress Cataloging-in-Publication Data

MacQueen, Graeme.
The 2001 anthrax deception : the case for a domestic conspiracy / by Graeme MacQueen.
pages cm
Includes bibliographical references and index.
ISBN 978-0-9860731-2-0
1. Bioterrorism--United States. 2. Anthrax--United States. 3. Postal service--United States. 4. Victims of terrorism--United States. I. Title.

HV6432.M332 2014
363.325'30973090511--dc23

2014029727

Clarity Press, Inc.
Ste. 469, 3277 Roswell Rd. NE
Atlanta, GA. 30305 , USA
http://www.claritypress.com

TABLE OF CONTENTS

ACKNOWLEDGEMENTS

I would like to offer my gratitude to Paul McArthur for organizing the first event in which I had the opportunity to talk publicly about the anthrax attacks. David Ray Griffin was a co-speaker at that event and I thank him for encouraging me, then and on subsequent occasions, to write up the results of my investigation.

Researchers who preceded me in the study of the anthrax attacks gave me prompt and generous assistance. Elias Davidsson and Barbara Honegger were ready to help. Meryl Nass read the manuscript carefully and gave detailed advice. Barry Kissin helped me at every stage of the research. He encouraged me, told me when he thought I was going off-track, and introduced me to sources of information that were new to me.

Philipp Sarasin's work was an essential source of inspiration, prompting me to look at aspects of the anthrax discourse I would otherwise have missed.

Herbert Jenkins read an early version of this book and offered constructive criticism. Elizabeth Woodworth carried out a detailed reading of several drafts and had much useful advice. She shared generously her own research materials and suggested I refashion into a book what was originally an academic article. Tod Fletcher copy-edited the manuscript twice and gently forced me to explain myself more fully, opening up my dense writing so that it would cause the reader fewer headaches. He also provided me with information that was new to me. I am very grateful to him.

I will not try to list all the friends and researchers who have supported my investigations over the years into the violent events of the fall of 2001, but I wish to give warm thanks to James Gourley, Laurie Manwell, Adnan Zuberi and Kevin Ryan, fellow members of the Steering Committee of the International Hearings on the Events of September 11, 2001. In his role as co-editor of the *Journal of 9/11 Studies*, as well as through his detailed investigations of the crimes of 9/11, Kevin Ryan continues to be an exceptional source of help and inspiration. I am grateful to Michael Keefer, Martha Nalband, Atif Kubursi, Rama Singh, Barrie Zwicker, Joanna Santa Barbara, Jack Santa Barbara, Sharon Mac-

Queen and Jessica MacQueen for fruitful conversations, new ideas and support.

I offer thanks and appreciation to all those who labor at the History Commons project, which has continued to provide a sound historical timeline available to everyone who carries out research on the events of the fall of 2001.

Diana Collier, Editorial Director of Clarity Press, has been a calm, sure guide, as well as an intellectual companion, throughout the process of expansion and revision of this manuscript.

CHAPTER 1

INTRODUCTION

In 2001, directly after the crimes of September 11, a series of events took place in the United States that are called the "anthrax letter attacks" or simply the "anthrax attacks." Although the casualties were few in comparison to those of 9/11, the implications of the anthrax attacks were more worrisome. Crashing planes into buildings is a crude method of attack and is less likely to produce very large numbers of casualties than dispersing a bioweapon such as anthrax. This was recognized in the fall of 2001 and there was a corresponding degree of concern.

I began looking into the anthrax attacks in 2010, having been led there by several years of study of the 9/11 attacks. Earlier, when I had examined the official story of 9/11, I encountered many surprises. More surprises were in store when I began to study the anthrax literature and to discuss the attacks with others. While the public remembers the 9/11 attacks vividly, I was perplexed by how quickly the anthrax attacks were disappearing from collective memory. I was surprised as well that almost no one I spoke to remembered the connections between the anthrax attacks and the 9/11 attacks. These connections were numerous. It gradually became clear why today neither the anthrax story as a whole nor its connections with 9/11 receives significant attention either from governments or the mainstream media: the documentary evidence relating to the anthrax attacks, when studied critically, raises serious questions not only about the FBI's account of the anthrax attacks but also about the U.S. government's account of what happened on September 11, 2001. Taken together, these sets of evidence erode the rationale for the Global War on Terror.

Much effort has been spent over the years deflecting attention from the weak foundations of the Global War on Terror, and several clever propaganda moves have been deployed to this end. My use of the term "conspiracy" in the title of this book provides a critical response to one such move. Both journalists and scholars have acceded to the thoughtless and pejorative use of the term "conspiracy" and the related term "conspiracy theory"[1] in relation to those who seek to question the official version of the events of 9/11. In doing so they have made honest and open discussion of key events purporting to justify the war on terror extremely difficult. Few people want to be dismissed as "conspiracy theorists"—even less as conspiracy "buffs," "nuts" and the like. So they quiet their doubts and try to believe what their governments tell them, however absurd the tales may be.

Many of the journalists and scholars using these terms in a propagandistic way seem to be unaware of what the expression has done to *them*. They have accepted the taboo implicit in the term; as it relates to 9/11, for 13 years they have refused to go into forbidden territory, convinced that this is a realm of enquiry that is polluted and dangerous and that only harm will come to them if they venture there. As a result many have not read the substantial critical literature of recent years: they know scarcely more about these "terrorist" events of the autumn of 2001 than they knew directly after the events took place. The "conspiracy theory" barrier has protected their worldview at the cost of keeping them, and the public whose interests they are supposed to serve, uninformed.

Perhaps it is not surprising that intellectuals keen to protect the U.S. government from criticism have tried to stigmatize "conspiracy theorists" and make their organizations objects of government infiltration and spying,[2] but it is disturbing to find those who are critical of the U.S. government working almost as hard to distance themselves from all talk of conspiracies. For example, in an otherwise insightful book on Islamophobia,[3] Stephen Sheehi says that conspiracy theories "are absurd manifestations of the illogic and contradictions within the ideology in which we live."[4] But when we read his account of the maintenance of Islamophobia in the U.S. we discover that people with great influence may join in a "cabal,"[5] "coterie,"[6] or "clique."[7] Members are bound by deep loyalties and exclude others from "the inner circle."[8] They make plans, and the plans sometimes result in immoral and illegal acts—including invasions of other countries. They do not hesitate to hold "secret meetings,"[9] even sometimes resorting to "undisclosed locations."[10] In a moment of forgetfulness, Sheehi even says they conspire.[11]

What is going on? Why are progressive thinkers like Sheehi determined, against the evidence they have themselves uncovered, to disparage conspiracy theories as legitimate avenues of enquiry—other than fear of career damage and job loss?

There seem to be three related misconceptions at the root of this confusion. First, people who write in this vein appear to think that if they acknowledge the existence of a particular conspiracy they can be seen as committing themselves to a whole string of conspiracies. Sheehi appears to feel that if one has a "conspiracy theory" of 9/11 (this is a misuse of the term, as I shall explain) one will necessarily believe in the Illuminati, as well as in theories having to do with Jews and One World Government.[12] But this is not so.

The second misconception can be seen as a continuation of the first. Some researchers appear to think that a person who holds a conspiracy theory with respect to a particular event must have a conspiratorial view of history—he or she must hold that history is nothing but the playing out of conspiracies. And, since it is easy to see that such a grand theory of history is false, all talk of conspiracies must be false. But, again, the reasoning is flawed. If I hold that the Black Death had a great impact on social life and changed history in important ways I am not committed to a "disease theory of history," according to which all of history is driven by epidemics. I am simply open to the reality of epidemic disease and its impacts on society and history. Why should I not be open to the existence of conspiracies and their impact on society and history?

A third misconception is the conviction that progress in thinking about human society and history has depended on rejecting the image of wizards behind the curtain controlling events. History, we are told, unfolds in ways that resist human will. Impersonal forces and random combinations of events drive history, and those who look for conspiracies represent a regression to a primitive or childish view of the world. But, once again, the choice presented is unnecessary. It is quite possible to acknowledge the power of forces of many kinds, as well as "ideological formations," the Political Unconscious, and so on, but none of this means that powerful people do not sometimes get together in confidence to plan destructive acts.

Unfortunately, the widespread unwillingness of intellectuals and journalists to acknowledge the reality of conspiracies has left civil society with little defense against the intelligence agencies and military structures—well funded and expert in deception and destruction—that currently pose a threat to democracies and to our human future.

Since much of the confusion and contradiction just discussed flourishes because of a failure to define terms, let me offer the definitions that underlie my work. A *conspiracy* is a plan made in secret, and involving more than one person, to commit an immoral or illegal act. A *conspiracy theory* is a theory that posits, or assumes the existence of, a conspiracy. These definitions may be simple but they honor normal usage and are of immediate help as we consider the violent events that took place in the U.S. in the fall of 2001.

Much time has been wasted on accusations that certain people hold a "conspiracy theory" about the events of September 11, 2001. Virtually everyone agrees that the crimes of that day were planned in secret by more than one person and that the aim was to carry out acts that, in the view of the great majority of humanity, were immoral and illegal. Therefore, there is universal or near universal agreement that the 9/11 events were the result of a conspiracy. We would have to look very hard to find anyone who does not hold a conspiracy theory about 9/11. And for this reason it is silly to denigrate people for holding a conspiracy theory about this event.

When the Warren Commission asked whether or not John Kennedy's assassination was the result of a conspiracy, it asked a good question. Kennedy's killing could have been the result of secret plans by either a "lone wolf" or a group. The Warren Commission certainly gave the wrong answer to its question,[13] but there was nothing wrong with the question. In the case of 9/11 the question is not a good one. No lone wolf option is available.

The anthrax attacks are, in this respect, closer to the Kennedy case than to the 9/11 attack on the Twin Towers. It appears, at least at first glance, to have been possible for the attacks to have been planned either by a lone wolf, as the FBI claims, or by a group. So the question as to whether or not the attacks were the result of a conspiracy—whether they involved more people than one—is a good one. When this book claims that the attacks were the result of a conspiracy it is saying something that is not obvious or trivial.

Of course, I am not merely claiming that the anthrax attacks were the result of a conspiracy but that they were the result of a domestic conspiracy—they resulted from planning by actors within the U.S. Moreover, I will be arguing that the conspiracy was not only domestic but undertaken at a high level: it cannot be pinned on skinheads or retail fascists but involved a group well placed in the executive branch of the U.S. government.

How can we settle such matters? How can we actually determine, in any given instance, whether or not a conspiracy has taken place and, if so, who the conspirators were? The tools of investigation are no different from those used to test other proposals. We use evidence and reason. In some cases we will be able to make confident assertions and in other cases we shall have to acknowledge that we are speculating, but even in this second case we will do our best to ground our speculation in evidence. Ideology, national loyalty, outrage and "common sense" will not do the job.

There is a large and complex literature on the anthrax attacks. I have attempted neither a comprehensive review of this literature nor a detailed account of the attacks. I want to draw attention to a quite specific set of difficulties raised by the evidence and, having done so, to argue in favor of the following points:

(a) The anthrax attacks were carried out by a *group* of perpetrators, not by a lone wolf.

(b) The group that perpetrated this crime included deep insiders within the U.S. executive branch.

(c) This group of perpetrators was linked to, or identical with, the perpetrators of the 9/11 attacks.

(d) The anthrax attacks were the result of a conspiracy meant to help redefine the enemy of the West, revising the global conflict framework from the Cold War to the Global War on Terror.

(e) The establishment of the Global War on Terror, to which the anthrax attacks contributed, enabled the U.S. executive branch to reduce the civil liberties of people in the U.S. and to attack other nations. Domestically and externally, these events were also used to weaken the rule of law.

A Note on the Hijackers

The alleged hijackers of four planes on September 11, 2001 play an important role in the anthrax story and will be mentioned frequently. To avoid repeated use of the word "alleged" or annoyingly frequent scare quotes ("the hijackers") I will capitalize the term: Hijackers. The term used in this way refers to the 19 Arabic-speaking men who are said, in the official account of 9/11, to have hijacked planes on 9/11. By capitalizing the term I indicate that these men played the *role* of hijacker in the scripted events leading up to September 11, 2001. I will give examples in Chapter 7 of the reasons many researchers doubt that these men in fact hijacked planes on September 11.

Endnotes

1 For an excellent discussion of conspiracy and its relation to political theory see Lance deHaven-Smith, *Conspiracy Theory in America* (Austin, Texas: Univ. of Texas Press, 2013).

2 Cass Sunstein and Adrian Vermeule, "Conspiracy Theories: Causes and Cures," *Journal of Political Philosophy* 17 (2009): 202–27. For a rebuttal of Sunstein and Vermeule, see David Griffin, *Cognitive Infiltration: An Obama Appointee's Plan to Undermine the 9/11 Conspiracy Theory* (Northampton, Mass.: Olive Branch Press, 2011).

3 Stephen Sheehi, *Islamophobia: The Ideological Case Against Muslims* (Atlanta: Clarity Press, 2011).

4 Ibid., 215.

5 Ibid., 57.

6 Ibid., 64.

7 Ibid., 50.

8 Ibid., 53, 64.

9 Ibid., 58.

10 Ibid., 54.

11 Ibid., 59.

12 Ibid., 215.

13 In my view, the fatal flaws of the Warren Commission's report were pointed out decades ago by its earliest critics. Readers may consult the website of the Mary Ferrell Foundation for an overview, bibliography and resources. "The JFK Assassination: Mary Ferrell Foundation," n.d., http://www.maryferrell.org/wiki/index.php/JFK_Assassination.

CHAPTER 2

THE 2001 ANTHRAX ATTACKS

The Disease

The term "anthrax" refers primarily to a disease.[1] But the term is also used to refer to the bacterium that causes the disease. There is, therefore, ambiguity in the expression, "anthrax attacks." The larger aim of the senders of the letters was to induce, or threaten to induce, the disease, but it is also true that spores of the bacterium were contained in some of the letters.

Like all bacteria, *Bacillus anthracis* (anthrax) is a single-celled microorganism. *B. anthracis* is also, however, a parasitic bacterium, meaning that it thrives on other life forms. *B. anthracis* has two main states, an active state, in which it can take in nutrients and reproduce, and a state of dormancy, in which there is no perceptible metabolic activity. Cells of the dormant form are referred to as "spores" or "endospores." The DNA inside the spore is protected from its environment by several layers of coating.

Spores of the genus *Bacillus* are among the hardiest type of cell that exists. Some are capable of surviving for thousands of years through drought and temperature extremes. The bacterium enters into this state of dormancy when nutrients are scarce, at which time the spores develop, through a complex, multi-phase process, within the vegetative cells and then separate themselves.

B. anthracis is found in the soil and in the bodies of animals, especially herbivores. Human beings, in natural conditions, generally take in spores indirectly via contact with animals. Since the spores are tough and can survive for long periods in the soil without water or nutrients, it is not easy to rid the soil of them. They remain ready to germinate when conditions are favorable—for example, within the body of a warm-blooded creature.

As a disease that afflicts human beings, anthrax takes three forms depending on the means by which the bacterium enters the body. If it enters through a cut in the skin, cutaneous anthrax results. The great majority of those who develop anthrax get this form of the disease. Swelling at the site of entry will eventually result in a black scab, from which the disease gets its name ("anthrax" is the Greek word for coal). Without treatment, about 20% of those who develop cutaneous anthrax will die; but it is easy to treat this form of the disease with antibiotics and in the modern period lethality rates are low. If the spores are ingested—for example, by eating undercooked meat containing anthrax spores—the result will be gastrointestinal anthrax, which has a much higher mortality rate than the cutaneous form. Finally, if the spores are breathed in the result is inhalation (or pulmonary) anthrax, which is the most lethal form of the disease: estimates of the lethality rate vary from 75% to 95%. All deaths in the 2001 attacks were the result of inhalation anthrax. That the rate of death was lower than normal in the 2001 attacks was probably due to widespread awareness of the disease (including foreknowledge and corresponding preparations) as well as prompt and intense treatment of people discovered to be infected.

In all forms of the disease antibiotics are crucial to treatment. The aim of antibiotics, after all, is to kill or impede the action of bacteria. But it is not the bacterium per se that is lethal but the toxins produced by the bacterium. If the victim's condition is not properly diagnosed and promptly treated—especially in the case of inhalation anthrax—even killing the bacteria with antibiotics will not stop the toxins from wreaking havoc on the body's organs.

When the inhalation form of the disease is first contracted symptoms are "flu-like:" sore throat, tiredness, mild fever, and so on. As the disease progresses the symptoms become more pronounced and may include difficulty in breathing, high fever, meningitis (swelling of the spinal cord and brain) and shock, followed by coma and death.

The Weapon

There is a long and sordid history of people deliberately inducing disease in other human beings through the introduction of bacteria, especially in the context of war and conquest. Many of the most devastating cases are pre-modern and involved such crude methods as hurling diseased corpses over walls.[2]

Because of its pathogenic nature and its ability to form durable spores, *B. anthracis* is a natural choice for those wishing to have a biological weapon. It has been developed as a weapon by nations over the last hundred years.[3]

Attempts were made by Germany in WWI to attack enemy livestock with anthrax bacteria.[4] Several other nations have produced and stored *B. anthracis*, though few have actually deployed it.

Although proponents of the Global War on Terror have devoted considerable energy to portraying the use of anthrax as "unthinkable" and as radically evil,[5] associating anthrax research and production with past adversaries of the United States such as the Soviet Union and Iraq, the Western nations were leaders in the development of biological weapons. During WWII Germany was ahead of the Allies in the development of chemical warfare but the United

Kingdom, the United States, and Canada were collaborating in the development of biological weapons and were well ahead of the Axis powers.[6] Near the end of WWII the Allies were in a position to launch a major anthrax attack on Germany. One plan involved dropping anthrax-infected cattle cakes to destroy beef and dairy herds, thus denying the German population major sources of food, while also dropping anthrax bombs on German cities to induce inhalation anthrax in humans. One estimate had these anthrax bombs taking the lives of three million people, most of them civilians.[7] Fortunately, although the weapons had been stockpiled and the delivery systems were in place, the attack was finally judged unnecessary. Germany's decision not to employ chemical and biological weapons directly against Allied forces and homelands was one factor in Allied restraint.[8] In addition, it was decided that if Germany could be brought to her knees without using these controversial weapons the Allies would be saved from condemnation by the many who found biological warfare repugnant.

The U.K. was the leader in anthrax research at the beginning of WWII but the U.S. led the way by the end, using its new Camp Detrick and Dugway testing ground. U.S. scientists quickly discovered how to produce large quantities of the bacterium, how to disperse it effectively (for example, through the use of aerosol bombs), and how to produce increasingly lethal subtypes of the bacterium.[9]

After WWII anthrax research and development continued, especially among the Cold War superpowers. The Soviet Union apparently retained a large and active program until the disintegration of the state.[10] In the U.S., Richard Nixon announced the termination of the U.S. biological program in 1969, putting faith instead in the U.S. nuclear arsenal. From that point on anthrax weapon development in the U.S. was curtailed and, to the extent that it survived, was forced to go underground.

Aerosolizing anthrax—causing large numbers of spores to be dispersed and suspended in the air—remains one of the most intensely studied, and most intensely feared, methods of biological warfare. It was central, both as a reality and as fiction, to the events of 2001.

Conventions and Acts

After WWI an initiative was mounted to ban the use of biological weapons, resulting in the Geneva Protocol of 1925. Its full name is "Protocol for the Prohibition of the Use in War of Asphyxiating, Poisonous or Other Gases, and of Bacteriological Methods of Warfare."[11] The U.S. was an early signatory but did not ratify the agreement until 1975.

The Geneva Protocol was an extension of earlier international agreements. It proclaims simply that the *use* of such weapons and methods is prohibited. It does not cover the development, stockpiling and sharing of such agents and methods.

In 1972 a new agreement, intended to remedy this deficiency, was presented to the world. Its common name is the "Biological Weapons Convention" (BWC), while its full name is "Convention on the Prohibition of the Development, Production and Stockpiling of Bacteriological (Biological) and Toxin Weapons and on their Destruction."[12] The BWC entered into force in 1975. It referred to, and built upon, the Geneva Protocol but carried the offensive against biological weapons to a new level by attempting to prohibit not merely their use but all necessary stages prior to deployment. The BWC makes it clear that the context of the agreement is the move toward "complete and general disarmament" and, especially, the "elimination of all types of weapons of mass destruction." The Convention explicitly seeks "to exclude completely the possibility of bacteriological (biological) agents and toxins being used as weapons."

One of the common complaints against international law is that it is too vague in what it prohibits and that it lacks adequate mechanisms for inspection and enforcement. The

BWC was an attempt to answer these objections by inching closer to an efficient, workable method of putting the ideals of the Geneva Protocol into effect.

In the 1980s some Americans were angry to learn that while government rhetoric had been blaming its enemies (Vietnam and the Soviet Union especially) for their research, and alleged deployment, of biological weapons, the U.S. itself was carrying out work that violated the BWC.[13] One of these critics was Harvard-trained international law expert, Professor Francis A. Boyle. Subsequently, Boyle himself was asked to draft the BWC's domestic enabling legislation.[14] The "Biological Weapons Anti-Terrorism Act of 1989" was adopted unanimously by both chambers of Congress, and George H. W. Bush signed it into law on May 22, 1990.[15]

Boyle has said that while he was willing to have the Act named as if it were directed against "Third World crazies" if that would make it palatable to Congress, his primary targets were actually the "crazies" in the U.S. military and intelligence communities.[16]

In 1995 participants from many countries began meeting to work out how to add verification procedures to the historic initiative to eliminate bio-weapons. The Protocol they worked out would have, they believed, provided transparency and made cheating much more difficult than it then was. The proposed agreement included on-site inspections of states that were parties to the BWC. On July 25, 2001, with international negotiations in high gear, the U.S. representative announced that the U.S. would not support the Protocol, implying that although the U.S. was trustworthy, other signatories were not and would continue to hide their biological weapons facilities. Although the U.S. was the only party to the Convention that did not support the Protocol, its support was considered crucial and the negotiations collapsed.[17]

The rejection of the Protocol by the George W. Bush administration was merely one result, among many, of that administration's strategy of weakening international law. The Protocol, of course, would also have made life much more difficult for anyone wishing to carry out the sort of anthrax attacks that occurred within the U.S. in the fall of 2001.

The Attacks

The anthrax attacks of 2001 began in September, shortly after the events of 9/11. [18] Victims of the attacks were identified between October 3 and November 20. At least 22 people were thought to have become infected, 11 with cutaneous anthrax and 11 with inhalation anthrax. All instances of the disease appear to have been caused by letters containing dried spores of the bacteria sent through the public mail. Two of those who died were postal workers.

The five people known to have died from anthrax (all from the inhalation form of the disease) were Robert Stevens, a Florida photo editor (died Oct. 5); Thomas Morris Jr., a postal worker at a mail sorting facility in Washington, D.C. (died Oct. 21); Joseph Curseen Jr., a postal worker at the same facility as Thomas Morris Jr. (died Oct. 22); Kathy Nguyen, a hospital employee in New York City (died Oct. 31); and Ottilie Lundgren, an elderly woman living in a small town in Connecticut (died Nov. 21).

The first letters to be recovered containing spores of *B. anthracis* were postmarked on September 18 in Princeton, New Jersey. Letters apparently sent at this time went to the following media corporations: NBC News, the *New York Post*, CBS News, ABC News, and the *Sun* (or possibly its sister publication, the *National Enquirer*). Infections were induced in all of these places. During this same period bio-threat letters containing messages and powder but no genuine anthrax were also sent to news media.

Beginning on approximately September 22, skin lesions began to develop in one or more persons at each of these news locations, but the illness was not yet diagnosed as anthrax.[19] Robert Stevens' illness was the first to be correctly diagnosed. Stevens was admitted to the hospital with an undiagnosed illness on October 2. His disease was diagnosed as anthrax on October 3 and a press conference was held announcing this on October 4. He died on October 5. Robert Stevens is exceptionally important in the history of the anthrax attacks not only because he was the first to die of the disease but also because no one, in the public or even the U.S. intelligence community, is supposed to have known that *B. anthracis* was in play before his diagnosis. That is, *according to the FBI, no one except the perpetrators knew before Oct. 3, 2001 that the attacks were in progress*. This date is important to keep in mind.

At some point between October 6 and October 8, letters containing a more highly refined and lethal preparation of *B. anthracis* were sent to Democratic Senators Thomas Daschle and Patrick Leahy.

Daschle's letter was opened and studied by the FBI on October 15. This single letter contaminated the Hart Senate Building, leading to the closure of the building and to numerous confirmed anthrax exposures. The Leahy letter was buried in mail that was sequestered after the discovery of the Daschle letter, so it was not discovered for some time.

The official U.S. government position immediately after the death of Stevens was that there was no evidence his death was part of a terrorist attack. However, the FBI soon opened a criminal investigation, and gradually the hypothesis became widespread that the attacks were the second blow in a "one-two punch" delivered by terrorists, the first blow having been the attacks of 9/11.

The "one-two punch" hypothesis is one among several that will be considered in the following chapters.

Endnotes

1 The brief description here is based on: Burke Cunha, "Anthrax," *Medscape*, n.d., http://emedicine.medscape.com/article/212127-overview; R. C. Spencer, "Bacillus Anthracis," *Journal of Clinical Pathology* 56

(2003): 182–87; Jesse Emspak, "How Anthrax Kills: Toxins Damage Liver and Heart," *Livescience*, August 28, 2013, http://www.livescience.com/39251-anthrax-kills-toxins-liver-heart.html.

2 Stefan Riedel, "Biological Warfare and Bioterrorism: A Historical Review," *Baylor University Medical Center Proceedings* 17 (4) (October 2004): 400–406.

3 My description is based on a critical reading of: John Bryden, *Deadly Allies: Canada's Secret War, 1937-1947* (Toronto: McClelland & Stewart, 1989); Jeanne Guillemin, *Biological Weapons: From the Invention of State-Sponsored Programs to Contemporary Bioterrorism* (New York: Columbia Univ. Press, 2005); Judith Miller, Stephen Engelberg, and William Broad, *Germs: Biological Weapons and America's Secret War* (New York: Simon & Schuster, 2001); Milton Leitenberg, "Biological Weapons: Where Have We Come from over the Past 100 Years?," *Public Interest Report: Journal of the Federation of American Scientists* 64, no. 3 (December 2011), http://www.fas.org/pubs/pir/article/bioweapons.html.

4 Guillemin, *Biological Weapons: From the Invention of State-Sponsored Programs to Contemporary Bioterrorism*, 21.

5 See Chapter 8.

6 Bryden, *Deadly Allies: Canada's Secret War, 1937-1947.*

7 Guillemin, *Biological Weapons: From the Invention of State-Sponsored Programs to Contemporary Bioterrorism*, 69.

8 Bryden, *Deadly Allies: Canada's Secret War, 1937-1947.*

9 Guillemin, *Biological Weapons: From the Invention of State-Sponsored Programs to Contemporary Bioterrorism*, 67 ff.

10 Ibid., 131 ff.

11 *Protocol for the Prohibition of the Use in War of Asphyxiating, Poisonous or Other Gases, and of Bacteriological Methods of Warfare*, 1925, http://www.un.org/disarmament/WMD/Bio/pdf/Status_Protocol.pdf.

12 *Convention on the Prohibition of the Development, Production and Stockpiling of Bacteriological (Biological) and Toxin Weapons and on Their Destruction*, 1972, http://disarmament.un.org/treaties/t/bwc/text.

13 Francis Boyle, *Biowarfare and Terrorism* (Atlanta: Clarity Press, 2005).

14 *Biological Weapons Anti-Terrorism Act of 1989*, 1990, http://thomas.loc.gov/cgi-bin/query/z?c101:S.993.ENR:.

15 Boyle, *Biowarfare and Terrorism.*

16 Ibid.

17 Rebecca Whitehair and Seth Brugger, "BWC Protocol Talks in Geneva Collapse Following U.S. Rejection," *Arms Control Association*, September 2001, https://www.armscontrol.org/print/900. For a somewhat different perspective, see Jonathan Tucker, "Biological Weapons Convention (BWC) Compliance Protocol," *NTI (Nuclear Threat Initiative)*, Aug. 1, 2001. http://www.nti.org/analysis/articles/biological-weapons-convention-bwc/

18 Information in this summary can be found in standard works on the

anthrax attacks such as Leonard Cole, *The Anthrax Letters: A Bioterrorism Expert Investigates the Attacks That Shocked America* (Skyhorse Publishing, 2009); Jeanne Guillemin, *American Anthrax: Fear, Crime, and the Investigation of the Nation's Deadliest Bioterror Attack* (New York: Henry Holt and Company, 2011); "History Commons: 2001 Anthrax Attacks."

19 "History Commons: 2001 Anthrax Attacks," September 22-October 2, 2001: Some People Get Sick from Anthrax, but Are Not Properly Diagnosed.

CHAPTER 3

WAR AND CIVIL LIBERTIES

The anthrax attacks occurred at a crucial moment in U.S. history. The attacks had to vie for space in the newspapers with several other important events. As October of 2001 progressed and more anthrax cases became known, the legislation that would eventually be called the USA PATRIOT Act ("Uniting and Strengthening America by Providing Appropriate Tools Required to Intercept and Obstruct Terrorism" Act) was being hurried through Congress. It was signed into law by George W. Bush on October 26. During this same month Bush gave his approval to the first bulk domestic spying by the NSA.

But in the fall of 2001 war overshadowed all else and enabled other transformations. The first U.S. military strike on Afghanistan took place two days after the first anthrax victim, Robert Stevens, died of inhalation anthrax in Florida. As the anthrax attacks developed, so did the invasion of Afghanistan. And in the background, preparations were underway for the invasion of Iraq.

It is important to reflect on the relationship between war and civil liberties, and on the steps that were taken in 2001 to ensure that a state of war was recognized so that the administration's goals could be achieved. Without understanding the role of war and the nature of the domestic preparations required to conduct it, we will not be in a position to understand the 2001 anthrax attacks.

War's Influence on Civil Liberties

War leaders, especially in recent history, have typically sought to achieve a high degree of social unity and public confidence in the executive during wartime. When mobilization begins the leadership seeks to ensure that there is no loss of energy or purpose, no doubt about the rectitude of the direction in which society is heading, no holding back from sacrifice. The entire social body is to cooperate. Although attempts to get the support of the general population have certainly been found in ancient times, the tendency to seek passionate, enthusiastic engagement during war became more common with the spread of republican forms of government and the replacement of professional armies with citizen armies.[1]

This desired unity and confidence in leadership can be, at times, a spontaneous development, but at other times propaganda has been necessary to help achieve the required "confidence in one's own cause and one's leaders."[2]

The social unity common in war does more than facilitate the use of force against an external enemy: it also reduces the space for dissent, and, therefore, the space for civil liberties, in the domestic population. As David Dodge put it, reflecting on what he saw around him in the U.S. during the war of 1812: "to inflame a mild republic with the *spirit of war* is putting all its liberties to the utmost hazard."[3]

A hundred years after Dodge, in a famous essay generally known as "War Is the Health of the State," Randolph Bourne recorded the process of mobilization in the U.S. as the nation joined WWI.[4] He noted that "it is precisely in war that the urgency for union seems greatest," and he observed that once an executive has made the decision to go to war the entire domestic population will commonly adopt the decision even if it was given little or no role in the process: "The moment war is declared...the mass of the people, through some spiritual alchemy, become convinced that they have willed and executed the deed themselves."

The people, said Bourne, "with the exception of a few malcontents, proceed to allow themselves to be regimented, coerced, deranged in all the environments of their lives, and turned into a solid manufactory of destruction." War "automatically sets in motion throughout society those irresistible forces for uniformity, for passionate cooperation with the Government in coercing into obedience the minority groups and individuals which lack the larger herd sense."

Where the executive sees insufficient uniformity it may simply crush dissent. Republics, Bourne claimed, can in times of war be difficult to distinguish from autocracies.

In short, during wartime the very liberties democracies claim to be fighting to protect are reduced. Whether these liberties will be regained depends on several factors, including the degree of persistence of a perceived external threat. References to the Global War on Terror as the "Long War," possibly lasting for generations, have naturally caused great concern among those who care about U.S. civil liberties.

The Case of 9/11

The Constitution of the United States explicitly gives to Congress the power to declare war. But the Constitution also says that the President will be Commander-in-Chief of the armed forces during war.[5] What was intended as a check and balance measure becomes a recipe for struggle. When taking on the role of Commander-in-Chief, presidents may demand certain powers—for decision-making and for deploying institutions arguably connected to war-making—that they normally do not have. Once a war is in motion, presidents keen on expanding their power can take advantage of the powers war grants them, and subsequent presidents can then cite these occasions as precedents for seizing further power.

In the case of 9/11, effort was expended from the very outset to define the day's attacks as an act of war, rather than simply an incident of terrorism. If the public were convinced that an act of war had taken place, if a condition of war was established, then it would seem natural for the U.S. government to respond within that framework. In that case—and especially if Congress gave some sign of approval—the President could arguably assume his role as Commander-in-Chief, and as embodiment of the executive branch of government, take whatever extraordinary powers he could assert were required.

During the day of September 11, as the television cameras rolled, one well-known personage after another proclaimed that the United States had been subjected to an act of war. (On CNN the list included John McCain, Curt Weldon, Samuel Berger, George Shultz, Shimon Peres, Lawrence Eagleburger, Orrin Hatch, James Woolsey, Dianne Feinstein and John Kerry.)[6] Yet when CNN anchor Judy Woodruff challenged Senator John McCain to justify the claim, the best he could do was to repeat his assertion.[7] Little wonder: it was not at all necessary to define the events as an act of war. Indeed, in light of the fact that no state seemed to have carried out the attacks, it was downright peculiar to call it an act of war, just as it was peculiar for the U.S. to consider carrying out an act of war in response. It would have been more natural to call the 9/11 events crimes and turn to either domestic U.S. law or international law for an appropriate response. The Taliban, who formed the *de facto* government in Afghanistan, indicated they would be willing to cooperate in a legal proceeding.[8] When Osama Bin Laden was accused of the deed by the U.S. government, they offered at various times to hand him over for trial if the U.S. would supply some evidence of his guilt. From the perspective of law this was an entirely reasonable request.

No credible evidence had been presented. Bin Laden had not been formally charged with the crime by the FBI (nor, for that matter, would he ever be charged for the crime of 9/11).[9] But on September 12 Bush publicly defined the 9/11 events as acts of war: "The deliberate and deadly attacks which were carried out yesterday against our country were more than acts of terror, they were acts of war."[10] The Bush administration had by this time already decided that war, not law, would be the framework used to deal with 9/11.

Bush did not even acknowledge the Taliban request for evidence as what it was. Instead, operating entirely within the discourse of war, he referred to Taliban requests as pleas for "negotiation," which he then declined.[11]

Secretary of State Colin Powell stated that the U.S. would soon be presenting, for the edification of the world, a document detailing evidence of Bin Laden's guilt.[12] When no such document was produced, the government of the United Kingdom stepped forward. The British document of October 4 was, however, astonishingly weak.[13] The preamble noted that, "this document does not purport to provide a prosecutable case against Osama Bin Laden in a court of law" even as it was purporting to provide something of much greater import: a *casus belli*. Indeed, the document consisted mainly of unverifiable claims from intelligence agencies, the evidence seldom rising to the level of circumstantial. Anthony Scrivener, Q.C., noted in *The Times* that, "it is a sobering thought that better evidence is required to prosecute a shoplifter than is needed to commence a world war."[14]

A familiar band of conservatives and neoconservatives rapidly made the point that since the attacks were an act of war, the U.S. must wage war in response. Henry Kissinger was among the first to make the point in writing. At about 9 p.m. on September 11 his article was posted online at the *Washington Post* site, and it showed up in print on September 12.[15] Evoking Pearl Harbor, Kissinger made it clear that treating the attacks as a police matter was not good enough.

The U.S. response must end "the way that the attack on Pearl Harbor ended—with the destruction of the system that is responsible for it." The U.S., Kissinger explained, should not confine its wrath to states connected, through evidence, to the 9/11 attacks: "any government that shelters groups capable of this kind of attack, whether or not they can be shown to have been involved in this attack, must pay an exorbitant price."

On September 12 others, almost as quick with their pens as Kissinger, joined the chorus. Robert Kagan, one of the founders of the neoconservative Project for the New American Century, began his article with another evocation of Pearl Harbor ("Sept. 11, 2001—the date that will live in infamy...") and then said that Americans must respond as did their grandfathers:[16]

> Not by engaging in an extended legal effort to arraign, try and convict killers, as if they were criminals and not warriors. But by doing the only thing we now can do: Go to war with those who have launched this awful war against us.

He continued: "Please let us make no mistake this time: We are at war now. We have suffered the first, devastating strike." And he urged that Congress "immediately declare war."

Neoconservative Charles Krauthammer was equally outspoken.[17] "This is not crime," he began his article. "This is war." He criticized Colin Powell for pledging to "bring those responsible to justice." You do not bring such people to justice, he said. "You bring criminals to justice; you rain destruction on combatants".

These suggestions may seem rather bold given the lack of evidence identifying a perpetrator, but Krauthammer claimed to know who the enemy was: "Our delicate sensibilities have prevented us from pronouncing its name...

Its name is radical Islam." After a few speculative comments about his chosen perpetrator, Krauthammer moved on to state sponsors. "And then there are the governments: Iran, Iraq, Syria and Libya among them. Which one was responsible? We will find out soon enough." Whatever state sponsor was unmasked, said Krauthammer, it too must be included in the U.S. war plan. "Any country that harbors and protects him [Bin Laden] is our enemy. We must carry the war to them." He finished his exercise by making the same point as Kagan: "We should seriously consider a congressional declaration of war."

Daniel Pipes, in the *Wall Street Journal*, September 12, noted that among the U.S. government failures that had permitted the attacks of the previous day, foremost had been "[s]eeing terrorism as a crime."[18] "The better approach," he claimed, "is to see terrorism as a form of warfare and to target not just those foot soldiers who actually carry out the violence but the organizations and governments that stand behind them."

On the same day and also in the *Wall Street Journal*, Mark Helprin excitedly pondered past aggressors who had stirred America's "ferocity," paying for it with "a Berlin that we had reduced to rubble" and "a Tokyo we had reduced to rubble."[19] He confidently named the chief suspects in the 9/11 attacks—Bin Laden, Saddam Hussein, Yasser Arafat—and concluded: "Let this spectacular act of terrorism be the decisive repudiation of the mistaken assumptions [sic] that conventional warfare is a thing of the past."

One day later, September 13, neoconservative academic Laurie Mylroie wrote an article for the *Wall Street Journal* ("The Iraqi Connection"), which, in a tangle of allegations and suggestions, furthered her project, which had begun several years previously, of laying the blame for terrorist attacks on the U.S. on Iraq.[20] She ended by asking whether terrorism against the U.S. cannot best be approached as: "acts of war, with all the complexity that wartime activities regularly involve?"

Is it not odd that all these intellectuals would risk urging such extreme actions against the wrong party? They were, after all, speaking in the absence of credible evidence. What if different perpetrators were shortly to be discovered or their identities were clarified by subsequent assaults on the U.S.? Why take the chance of losing your credibility by going after those who might very shortly turn out to be the wrong people? Were these accusers all simpletons, or were they parties, knowingly or not, to a plan that preceded 9/11? That they may have shared a predilection for accusing Muslims (whether Muslims were complicit or not) is not so surprising; that they united in calling for war as the appropriate response should give pause.

The process continued. On September 14, a *Washington Post* article by John Lancaster and Susan Schmidt noted: "Stunned by the magnitude of Tuesday's terrorist attacks, Congress and the White House are reassessing an approach to fighting terrorism that until this week has favored the tools of law enforcement over those of war."[21] The intellectual framework for endorsing a policy of war was almost complete.

On September 12 Bush had met with Congressional leaders to explain the need for a resolution that would allow him to use force.[22] Democratic Senator Tom Daschle indicated at that meeting that he was willing to step up and propose the bill to Congress. Since he was Senate Majority Leader that virtually guaranteed its acceptance. He did not, however, write the text of the bill: it was forwarded to him by the White House that evening. Despite his eagerness to be of help, Daschle was taken aback by the breadth of the resolution. It was not a full-fledged declaration of war but it gave the President of the United States extraordinary power and breadth of action. After a preamble the text read:

> That the President is authorized to use all necessary means and appropriate force

> against those nations, organizations, or persons he determines planned, authorized, harbored, committed, or aided in the planning or commission of the attacks against the United States that occurred on September 11, 2001, and to deter and preempt any related future acts of terrorism or aggression against the United States.[23]

Daschle understood that this resolution would give a "blank check to go anywhere, anytime, against anyone the Bush administration or any subsequent administration deemed capable of carrying out an attack."[24] So he had the resolution modified. The final resolution, after an expanded preamble, said:

> That the President is authorized to use all necessary means and appropriate force against those nations, organizations, or persons he determines planned, authorized, committed or aided the terrorist attacks that occurred on September 11, 2001, or harbored such organizations or persons, in order to prevent any future acts of international terrorism against the United States by such nations, organizations or persons.[25]

Daschle had managed, through his revisions, to restrict permission for future aggression by keeping the focus more tightly on the September 11 events. But the resolution still had two profoundly important implications beyond the obvious facilitation of an attack on Afghanistan. First, this resolution arguably (not everyone agreed) let Bush assume the role of Commander-in-Chief, and that meant he would now be able to use his new special powers in ways that could have profound effects domestically. This, as we shall see, is what he immediately began to do. Second, there were crucial *epistemic* implications—implications having to do with knowledge and the validation of knowledge—of this resolution. The resolution gave Bush the right to determine *matters of fact* in relation to the events of 9/11: he got to say who planned, carried out, and so forth, the 9/11 attacks. Although he could call on U.S. intelligence agencies to help him, there was no requirement that their methods meet the standards of a legal process. George Bush could have determined that the Tooth Fairy was responsible for 9/11 and still have met the conditions of the resolution. This was a fatal mistake on the part of Congress.

On September 14 the revised resolution was proposed to, and approved by, both chambers of Congress. Democratic Representative Barbara Lee (in later years the Chair of the Congressional Black Caucus) cast the sole vote in Congress against the resolution. On September 18 Bush signed the bill into law.

Pollsters immediately got to work to determine how willing the public was, directly after the 9/11 assaults, to support military force while surrendering civil rights. A *Washington Post*-ABC poll was initiated on the evening of 9/11.[26] The poll reportedly found that "nearly nine in 10 people supported taking military action against the groups or nations responsible for yesterday's attacks even if it led to war. Two in three were willing to surrender 'some of the liberties we have in this country' to crack down on terrorism."

The Tribunals

Having induced Congress to approve the use of force, the executive kept up its momentum and, with the help of the anthrax attacks, put in place the systems that would reduce the civil liberties of everyone in the United States. And immediately after the Patriot Act and the NSA domestic spying were in place (this is discussed in the next chapter), the executive announced its intention to set up a special system of military tribunals to try people seized in the Global War on Terror.

In November and early December of 2001 the Senate Judiciary Committee held three days of hearings in which the proposed military tribunals were the central focus.[27] Patrick Leahy, Chair of the Committee, noted that although he had been in daily contact with the Department of Justice during the negotiations leading to passage of the Patriot Act, no one from the DOJ had mentioned to him the setting up of military tribunals.[28] He was concerned, and he saw it as his committee's duty to look into the matter.

During the hearings many expert witnesses challenged the executive's right to establish the tribunals, especially in view of the fact that the U.S. Constitution gives that power to Congress.

Neal Katyal, for example, Professor of Law at Georgetown University, said that what was taking place was clearly a seizure of power. "The Executive Branch is acting as lawmaker, law enforcer, and judge."[29]

To challenges such as Katyal's, various responses were given by those witnesses who supported the proposed tribunals, but they all boiled down to some variation of the claim that the U.S. was at war and that the executive was entitled to special powers during war.

Michael Chertoff, then Assistant Attorney General, Criminal Division, Department of Justice, was the first witness to appear at the hearings on behalf of the DOJ. "We are at war," he explained.[30] "We are dealing with a power that the President is exercising that comes from his status as Commander-in-Chief and not his status as head of the law-enforcement function."[31]

When Attorney General Ashcroft made a reluctant, scowling appearance on the last day of the hearings, he made the same point: "the Constitution vests the President with the extraordinary and sole authority as Commander-in-Chief to lead our Nation in times of war."[32]

William Barr, former Attorney General of the United States, added his weight:

> ...the President is acting as Commander-in-Chief of our armed forces—he is exercising the war powers of the United States. Our national goal in this instance is not the correction, deterrence and rehabilitation of an errant member of the body politic; rather, it is the destruction of foreign force that poses a risk to our national security.[33]

Any reader of the hearings transcripts will quickly understand that the assault on civil liberties in the U.S. that began subsequent to the 9/11 attacks was entirely dependent on the claim that the country was at war. The separate ideas customarily contained in this claim were: the attacks on New York and Washington were acts of war; the U.S. was, from the moment of those attacks, in a *de facto* state of war which it could not avoid; the September 14 resolution on the use of force by Congress recognized these facts and gave the Congressional approval that allowed the President to become Commander-in-Chief. Every one of these separate claims can be disputed, but the fact remains that the notion that the U.S. was at war—and that it had come to this condition justly and as a victim—was central to the U.S. government's initiatives, both internal and external, in the fall of 2001.

A legal proceeding is supposed to lead to a just decision, and it cannot do this unless it is able to uncover the truth. Both the pretrial stages of the procedure and the trial itself find their justification in truth. The relationship of the war system to evidence and truth is not at all the same. War leaders want social unity. They want everyone to get behind them. If telling the population the truth helps achieve social unity under the command of the executive, then the truth will be told; and if it has the opposite effect, as it will in many cases, it frequently will be avoided, hidden or distorted.

Choosing the war system rather than the legal system has, therefore, grave implications. If law is chosen official prosecutors will be obligated to provide evidence and to provide a chain of reasoning that connects the evidence to the criminal charge. If either the evidence or the argument fails, conviction is not possible. (Of course, in the real world the process is imperfect, but this is the formal aim of the process and this is how we judge whether or not the legal process is unfolding as it should.) War is a different sort of system altogether. When George W. Bush said he was going to respond to the events of 9/11 with war he was signaling that the process of seeking and evaluating evidence appropriate to the legal system would not be in operation.

As for the tribunals proposed by the executive, they were to be designed and established by the Secretary of Defense (Donald Rumsfeld), and, in accordance with this, were subordinated to the war system and lacked the truth-finding obligations of a legal proceeding. Charles Siegel, in a submission on behalf of the Human Rights Committee of the American Branch of the International Law Association, wrote the following about the proposed military commissions:

> Every single Constitutional guarantee intended to prevent the conviction and punishment of the innocent is deliberately sacrificed in the design of the Commissions. There is no indictment by grand jury, no jury trial, no presumption of innocence, no privilege against self-incrimination, no public trial, no right to counsel of the defendant's choosing, no right to confront the evidence against one, no right to trial by an independent and impartial judge, no right to be convicted only by proof beyond a reasonable doubt. Conviction and death sentence may be imposed by two-thirds of the hand-picked

> commission members. There is no appeal. There are no rules of evidence.[34]

Critics of the proposed tribunals who made submissions to the Senate hearings appear to have been mystified. Why use a process that was so flawed in its ability to discover the truth that it was almost certain to convict the wrong people?[35] Not only would innocent people languish in prison, but the guilty would remain at large, free to plan further acts of violence against the United States. Moreover, by putting to one side a tried and respected legal system in favor of a system helpless to discover the truth, the administration would be held in contempt by allies in the Global War on Terror, who might respond by withholding their cooperation.[36] This particular executive power seizure seemed not only illegitimate but perverse. How would it favor the war plans of the executive?

Timothy Edgar, Legislative Counsel at the Washington National Office of the American Civil Liberties Union, wrote:

> The right to a trial by a jury of one's peers, presided over by an impartial judge, also helps ensure a process designed to arrive at the truth, not at a pre-ordained conclusion.
>
> Without enforcement of these rights, the government may focus on the wrong people, and even obtain convictions of innocent people, while the terrorists go free to engage in more acts of terror.[37]

Edgar's insight was surprisingly rare in submissions to the hearings, and it is not clear that even he realized the extent to which the truth was in peril. If the entire narrative of Bin Laden and his 19 men was fiction, and if key members of the executive branch knew this and wished to keep this truth hidden, would it not be *essential* to construct a system of tribunals entirely obedient to the executive and entirely impotent to discover the truth? This possibility seems to have been too sinister even for most critics of the administration to foresee or entertain.

There were some in the aftermath of the 9/11 events who understood that the process of truth-seeking was in peril. Two days after the attacks Francis Boyle, professor of international law at the University of Illinois, was interviewed on FOX News channel by Bill O'Reilly.[38] Refusing to endorse a war in Afghanistan, Boyle said: "We have to look at this very rationally. This is a democracy. We have a right to see what the evidence is and proceed in a very slow and deliberate manner." O'Reilly replied: "No, we don't. We do not, as a republic, we don't have the right to see what the evidence is if the evidence is of a national security situation."

Boyle was insistent. Before he would endorse a war with anyone, he said:

> I want to see the evidence that we are relying on to justify this. So far, I do not see it. I see allegations. I see innuendo. I see winks and I see nods, but I do not see the evidence that you need under international law and the United States constitution so far to go to war. Maybe that evidence will be there, but it is not there now.

Boyle was prepared to speak of the possibility of war, but only if war was constrained by, and understood within, the framework of law. For this he received not just O'Reilly's denunciation, but hate mail and a public repudiation by the Dean of his law school.[39] Clearly, law was out and war was in. The U.S. executive did not hesitate to seize the opportunity.

Endnotes

1 A key work in the evolution of modern war is Carl Von Clausewitz, *On*

War, ed. Anatol Rapoport, trans. J. J. Graham (Baltimore: Penguin, 1968). This work, still unfinished at the author's death in 1831, recognized the energy and power of the citizen army fired with zeal and purpose. Clausewitz had personally witnessed the French citizen armies of his time defeating the professional standing armies of other European nations, and he was keen to set down the lessons of the experience.

2 Sidney Rogerson, *Propaganda in the Next War* (New York: Garland Publishing, 1972; originally published in 1938), 11.

3 Peter Brock, ed., *The First American Peace Movement* (New York: Garland Publishing, 1972), 32.

4 Randolph Bourne, "The State ('War Is the Health of the State')," 1918, http://www.antiwar.com/bourne.php.

5 "Constitution of the United States," http://www.archives.gov/exhibits/charters/constitution_transcript.html.

6 CNN same-day coverage of September 11, 2001. This footage appears to be available only sporadically on the internet. The author has depended on his own copy of the full CNN same-day coverage.

7 The McCain-Woodruff interaction occurred slightly after 12:30 p.m.

8 "History Commons: Complete 911 Timeline," September 13, 2001: Taliban Says Bin Laden Denies Role in 9/11. The theme continues and is documented in the Complete 911 Timeline. http://www.historycommons.org/project.jsp?project=911_project.

9 Bianca May and Morgan Ulery, "No Hard Evidence Connecting Bin Laden to 9/11," *Project Censored*, April 28, 2010, http://www.projectcensored.org/16-no-hard-evidence-connecting-bin-laden-to-9-11/; "FBI: No Evidence Osama Behind 9/11," *KSLA News* (Los Angeles: KSLA News 12, October 25, 2006), https://www.youtube.com/watch?v=B_6tpY2f35A.

10 "History Commons: Context of 'September 12, 2001: Bush Calls 9/11 Attacks "Acts of War,"'" n.d., http://www.historycommons.org/context.jsp?item=a091201actsofwar.

11 "Exchange [of G. W. Bush] With Reporters on Returning From Camp David, Maryland," October 14, 2001, http://www.gpo.gov/fdsys/pkg/WCPD-2001-10-22/pdf/WCPD-2001-10-22-Pg1477-2.pdf.

12 "History Commons: Complete 911 Timeline," September 23-24, 2001: Secretary of State Powell Says White House Will Provide Evidence of Al-Qaeda Role in 9/11, but He Is Contradicted by White House.

13 *Responsibility for the Terrorist Atrocities in the United States* (London, U.K.: British Government, October 4, 2001), http://news.bbc.co.uk/2/hi/uk_news/politics/1579043.stm.

14 Anthony Scrivener, "Evidence Would Not Stand up in a Court," *The Times*, October 5, 2001.

15 Henry Kissinger, "Destroy the Network," *Washington Post*, September 12, 2001; I. Berg, "Henry the Great on September 11," April 2002, http://www.dailybattle.pair.com/2010/henry-the_great_on_september_11.shtml.

16 Robert Kagan, "We Must Fight This War," *The Washington Post*, September 12, 2001.

17 Charles Krauthammer, "To War, Not to Court," *The Washington Post*, September 12, 2001.

18 Daniel Pipes, "Mistakes Made the Catastrophe Possible," *Wall Street Journal*, September 12, 2001.

19 Mark Helprin, "We Beat Hitler. We Can Vanquish This Foe, Too," *Wall Street Journal*, September 12, 2001.

20 Laurie Mylroie, "The Iraqi Connection," *Wall Street Journal*, September 13, 2001.

21 John Lancaster and Susan Schmidt, "U.S. Rethinks Strategy for Coping With Terrorists; Policy Shift Would Favor Military Action, Tribunal Over Pursuing Suspects Through American Courts," *The Washington Post*, September 14, 2001.

22 Tom Daschle and Michael D'Orso, *Like No Other Time: The 107th Congress and the Two Years That Changed America Forever* (New York: Crown Publishers, 2003), 122 ff.

23 Ibid., 123.

24 Ibid.

25 *Authorization for Use of Military Force*, 2001, https://www.govtrack.us/congress/bills/107/sjres23.

26 Richard Morin, "Almost 90% Want U.S. To Retaliate, Poll Finds," *The Washington Post*, September 12, 2001.

27 *Department of Justice Oversight: Preserving Our Freedoms While Defending Against Terrorism* (Washington, D.C., 2002), http://www.gpo.gov/fdsys/pkg/CHRG-107shrg81998/pdf/CHRG-107shrg81998.pdf.

28 Ibid., 15.

29 Ibid., 97.

30 Ibid., 14.

31 Ibid., 55.

32 Ibid., 313.

33 Ibid., 62.

34 Ibid., 465.

35 Ibid., 2.

36 Ibid., 3.

37 Ibid., 376.

38 FOX News, The O'Reilly Factor, Sept. 13, 2001.

39 Private correspondence with Francis Boyle.

CHAPTER 4

ANTHRAX AND CIVIL LIBERTIES

The events of 9/11 left many Americans shaken. Into this atmosphere of depression and upset came worries about anthrax.[1] As will be explained later, worries about anthrax actually preceded October 3, the date of confirmation of the first anthrax attack. That is, people had already become concerned about anthrax before the news about the anthrax attacks became public. Many began taking Ciprofloxacin, the antibiotic favored at the time for anthrax, and there was open discussion of the need for a publicly available anthrax vaccine. By September 26, even though, according to the official story, no one but the perpetrators knew anthrax had been released in the mails, there were open discussions in the press of an "anthrax scare."[2] After the death of Robert Stevens on October 5, the fears had a sound basis and grew rapidly.

The U.S. media did not hesitate to make anthrax fears a major theme. In fact, they considered fears of anthrax almost as newsworthy as anthrax itself and reported on them repeatedly. By reporting on these fears, they participated, of course, in their spread. "Anxiety" was probably the most common term ("Anthrax Anxiety at Home,"[3] "widespread anxiety in New York,"[4] "Anxiety Grows in South Florida,"[5] "Anxiety Over Bioterrorism Grows"[6]), but there were also references to "a frightened public,"[7] "rising public concern,"[8] "panicky citizens"[9] and "hysteria."[10] There were also references to "jitters"[11] and "nervousness."[12] Immediately after the death of Robert Stevens, the *Washington Post* reported that "jittery" citizens were "on their knees begging for drugs."[13] On October 10 the appropriately named Darryl Fears reported in the same newspaper that after law enforcement agencies put the nation in a state of high alert and Ashcroft asked Americans to maintain "a heightened state of awareness," the result was increased fear.[14] Along with the demand for Cipro, it appears, there was now a demand for gas masks.[15] Soon (Oct. 15) it was reported that the "anthrax scare" was spreading around the world.[16] Eventually (Oct. 18) the reading public was informed that "the fear of anthrax has become inescapable,"[17] and shortly thereafter—not long before the final Congressional votes on the Patriot Act—Americans were said to be experiencing "primordial terror"[18] in "a national anxiety attack."[19] It did not take long for journalists to come up with a clever aphorism: anthrax is not contagious, but *fear* of anthrax is.[20]

But ordinary citizens were not the only ones who had been targeted. The U.S. Congress was in the crosshairs as well. The targeting of Congress appeared to have started on 9/11. Senator Tom Daschle recalls being at the U.S. Capitol when he and other members of Congress were interrupted by the news of the 9/11 attacks.[21] They began watching events unfold on television like everyone else. Daschle says that not long after the incident at the Pentagon (roughly 10:38 a.m.) a Capitol police officer ran into the room. "Senator," he said, "we're under attack. We have word that an airplane is heading this way and could hit the building anytime. You need to evacuate."[22]

The view that the plane that was ultimately destroyed in Pennsylvania ("Flight 93") was headed for the Capitol was common at the time. For members of Congress the existence of this plane signified that they had been the target of a direct attack aimed at mass casualties and that only good fortune had saved them.

Daschle remembers that "the scene was total chaos." "The halls," he says, "were filled with fear and confusion." It was "the first time in history that the entire United States Capitol had been evacuated."[23] With no procedure in place for this particular type of attack, senators and representatives scattered. Daschle, as Senate Majority Leader, was put by his security detail into a helicopter and flown to a "secure location." Later, in the evening, some members of Congress drifted back to the Capitol, where the assembled crowd stood on the steps of the Capitol, listened to speeches, and broke into a spontaneous rendition of God Bless America.[24]

That the unity created by threat and war was already taking hold is clear from Daschle's comments: "we turned to one another like long-lost members of a large family and embraced."[25] Of the day as a whole, he remarks: "I can't think of a time in my life when I have witnessed such deeply felt unity and connection among our countrymen."[26]

Polls soon confirmed Daschle's observations. A sense of national unity and pride increased, support for the executive dramatically climbed, and citizens confirmed a willingness to surrender some of their civil liberties as part of the sacrifice that seemed demanded of them.[27]

From that violent day in September until the anthrax attacks were finished, there was no time when Congress was able to feel safe. After 9/11 the Capitol was closed to the public and "surrounded by yellow police tape and concrete barriers."[28] The danger of further violent incidents, especially directed at Congress, became a major media theme during the remainder of the fall.

On October 2, a day before the diagnosis of Stevens' disease, U.S. intelligence sources told Congress that if the U.S. conducted military strikes against Afghanistan (which it had every intention of doing and which it began doing five days later) there was a "100% chance" of a terrorist attack by Bin Laden's group. Expected targets, said the intelligence officials, included symbols of culture such as "government buildings in Washington." Biological or chemical weapons were said to be leading worries.[29]

On October 6, after Stevens had died but before his death was known to have been the result of an intentional criminal act, the *Washington Post* reported that "many of the nation's premier monuments" (this certainly would have included key Washington locations) were "targets of opportunity" for biological and chemical terrorism.[30]

On October 9 it was noted that terrorist retaliation was expected now that the bombing of Afghanistan had begun, and that Congress was considered a prime target. Members of Congress were advised to hide their identities. "On Capitol Hill members of Congress were discouraged from wearing their congressional pins when they are away from the Capitol." Moreover, they were "advised for security reasons to avoid using license plates or anything else that would identify them as members of Congress."[31]

On October 10 it was learned that "concern over an attack on the U.S. Capitol" was resulting in a variety of proposals for road closings and barriers. "Washington is considered one of the leading targets for terrorists."[32] Funds were sought for emergency preparedness.[33] On the same day it was learned that Capitol police were barring trucks and buses from proximity to the Capitol.[34]

On October 11 the FBI issued its most specific threat warning since 9/11, saying that "additional terrorist acts could be directed at U.S. interests at home and abroad over the 'next several days.'" The warning included all types of terrorist attacks and specifically mentioned the Capitol as a possible target. Mention was made of danger from crop-dusters, raising the possibility of biological or chemical attacks by this means. Moreover, Ari Fleischer "said the decision to issue the alert is consistent with Bush's insistence that federal authorities immediately release information about anthrax cases in Florida."[35]

This FBI warning of October 11 came directly before the crucial discussion and vote in Senate on the Patriot Act. The bill was passed late in the evening of October 11.

The Strategy of Tension?

Anxiety, fears, warnings by intelligence agencies: these dogged members of Congress throughout the fall of 2001. Were they the result of international terrorism of the al-Qaeda variety? Or did they issue from the heart of the U.S. state itself? If the latter, could they have come from a group that was intentionally intimidating Congress? Although the term "terrorism" would still be applicable in this case, more precision can be achieved by employing the academically recognized concept of "strategy of tension."

For several decades in post-WWII Europe a program of fear and intimidation was mounted by members of European security services working with non-state and international allies, including the CIA and NATO. The most common name for the general program is GLADIO, meaning "Sword," the name originally given to the Italian version of the program. The strategy of tension was central to GLADIO. GLADIO scholar Daniele Ganser explains it as follows:

> In its essence, the strategy of tension targets the emotions of human beings and aims to spread maximum fear among the target group. 'Tension' refers to emotional distress and psychological fear, whereas 'strategy' refers to the technique of bringing about such distress and fear. A terrorist attack in a public place, such as a railway station, a market place, or a school bus, is the typical technique...After the attack—and this is a crucial element—the secret agents who carried out the crime blame it on a political opponent...[36]

The strategy of tension as a subcategory within psychological warfare was employed in post-WWII Europe both to arouse antagonism towards selected groups and to induce the fearful population (as well as targeted members of elected state bodies) to take refuge in, and cede power to, the state's security apparatus. As a powerful tool of the political Right, it was employed to discredit members of the Left and, in some countries, to put in peril the project of liberal democracy. It served both to arouse hatred toward a designated and framed Other and to achieve public consent to the reduction of the civil liberties of the population on which it was unleashed.

The present book makes the case that the 2001 anthrax attacks were products of a domestic conspiracy initiated by parties in high positions within the U.S. state. I contend that the conspirators utilized the strategy of tension while framing a Muslim Other (al-Qaeda and Iraq), to push the American population and its elected representatives into a form of civic self-immolation: frightened, they ceded liberties and powers.

Passing the Patriot Act

In the case of the Patriot Act, our investigation requires attention to details of targets and timing. As a brief review of the passing of the Patriot Act will show, the peculiar convergence, already noted, of the October 11 FBI warning and the passing of the Patriot Act by Senate, is merely one instance of such convergences.

We may begin with two questions about the anthrax attacks on Congress. If the anthrax attacks were products of the strategy of tension, why target the Senate, as opposed to the House of Representatives? And, why target two particular senators—Tom Daschle and Patrick Leahy?

There is no mystery as to why the Senate was targeted rather than the House of Representatives. In the House the Republicans had a comfortable majority. It was almost impossible for the Patriot Act to fail in the House. But the Senate, through a number of accidents, had ended up with a Democratic majority. It was a majority of one, but still a majority. If Democrats decided to reject the bill, and if they voted as a bloc, the bill would fail. The Senate vote was essential: both chambers had to pass the bill before it could become law.

The question of why these two senators were targeted is only slightly more complicated. Tom Daschle (Democrat, South Dakota) was Senate Majority Leader. In his role as, arguably, the most powerful Democrat in the Senate, Daschle would have been expected to help direct debate in the Senate and to establish a timetable for the discussion and passing of the new legislation supposedly crafted to deal with terrorism. During this process he would also be expected to consult with both the opposition party and members of the executive.[37] Given the Democratic majority in the Senate, he was crucial to the passing of the new legislation.

Patrick Leahy (Democrat, Vermont) was Chairman of the Senate Judiciary Committee. This committee is a standing committee of the Senate, which has as one of its mandated duties the consideration of all legislation relating to civil liberties.[38] Leahy's committee was only one of several that reviewed the proposed Patriot Act, but it was the most important given the direct relationship of the legislation to civil liberties. In fact, Leahy played a central role throughout the discussion and refinement of the bill.

The U.S. Senate is supposed to be a body of "wise elders" and is expected to behave carefully and with deliberation. But under constant bullying by John Ashcroft and other members of the executive branch, this body acted much more quickly than it normally would have with important new legislation. Journalist John Lancaster, for example, noted the "blistering pace of the legislation through Congress" and the extreme dissatisfaction some members of Congress felt after what they judged to be a failure of democratic process.[39]

In one sense, then, given Democratic control of the Senate and the importance of quickly getting these two senators on board, it is obvious why Daschle and Leahy would be key targets of intimidation for anyone wanting the bill passed. The real question is why, given the clear desire of these two senators to cooperate with both the executive and the opposition party, someone would have felt it necessary to intimidate them.

Recall that Daschle felt an overwhelming sense of the unity of the American people after the 9/11 attacks. He was the one who willingly proposed the crucial resolution on the use of force on September 14 that began the process of handing over power to the executive. Reading accounts of these events today, we do not readily conclude that Daschle was an obstreperous figure needing a lethal threat.

Similar things can be said about Mr. Leahy. He believed in the necessity of the Patriot Act and he worked day and night, in consultations with John Ashcroft and other members of the executive, to refine the legislation so that it could be passed with as little delay as possible.

But what may look to us, in retrospect, as passivity in the face of the executive seizure of power may at the time have appeared to the administration as dangerous resistance. Moreover, it is important to bear in mind that although events such as the 9/11 attacks can induce people to sacrifice their civil rights, the effect appears to be time limited.[40] Those wishing to push through draconian legislation will know they must do it quickly, before the psychological effects of the initial event wear off.

While Leahy and Daschle were in favor of some form of the Patriot Act, there were issues over which they drew the line. Inevitably, this slowed down the process. To someone concerned to see the legislation enacted promptly there would always linger the possibility that the Senate, under the guidance of people committed to civil liberties, might begin acting in a genuinely deliberative way and reject or gut the new legislation, as Congress had done when similar and related legislation had been put forward after the Oklahoma bombing of 1996.[41]

From this perspective, it would seem that October 2 was the day the two senators put themselves at risk of death. Here is a quick review of events leading to that day.

On Monday, September 17, Attorney General John Ashcroft first publicly announced he would be sending an "antiterrorism" proposal to Congress. He made it clear at that time that he wanted it enacted with blazing speed: "we will be working diligently over the next day or maybe two to finalize this comprehensive proposal, and we will call upon the Congress of the United States to enact these important antiterrorism measures this week."[42] If Daschle had been shocked by the draft of the use of force proposal that he received on September 12, he was now shocked again. Ashcroft's draft of the Patriot Act was, it turned out, not even presented to Congress until Wednesday, September 19. Was Congress really supposed to pass this complex, lengthy and extremely important legislation between Wednesday the 19th and Friday the 21st with no significant review whatsoever?[43]

This request went too far. Leahy, wanting to cooperate but unwilling to see Congress "rubber-stamp the anti-terrorism proposals" said that "[i]f the Constitution is shredded, the terrorists win."[44] He added that he would work hard over the weekend and, with luck, be prepared to have a more acceptable draft ready by Tuesday, September 25, at which time his committee would hold hearings on the bill. Leahy's tone was positive. He said, according to the *Washington Post* (September 20), that he hoped "that Congress could send the anti-terrorism measure to President Bush within a few weeks—an expedited schedule that reflects the continuing sense of national emergency."[45] "A few weeks" was, indeed, a greatly accelerated schedule, but it was not sufficiently accelerated for the Bush administration.

Ashcroft had stressed the continuing emergency and the ongoing pressing danger of terrorism when he announced his bill, and he would reiterate this many times. The need for the rapid passage of the legislation was a constant theme in his speeches during this period.[46]

In Tom Daschle's words, Ashcroft "attacked Democrats for delaying passage of this bill." "[I]n this climate of anxiety, the attorney general was implicitly suggesting that further attacks might not be prevented if Democrats didn't stop delaying."[47]

Meanwhile, opposition to the bill was rapidly growing, both inside Congress and among a broad variety of civil society groups concerned about the proposed inroads on civil liberties.[48] But the administration kept up the pressure. In an important September 20 speech Bush took the opportunity to mention the importance of the new legislation.[49]

By September 22 rumors of biological terrorism had begun to spread in the mass media, and shortly thereafter the rumors included suggestions that al-Qaeda might conduct mass attacks with crop-dusting planes.[50] This added to the atmosphere of tension.

But the legislation had run into trouble. On Monday, September 24, it came in for criticism in committees of both the Senate and House. Leahy kept working to construct an acceptable bill by Tuesday, September 25, while Ashcroft kept pushing. "Terrorism is a clear and present danger to Americans today," he said, adding that "each day that so passes is a day that terrorists have an advantage."[51] On September 25 questions and criticisms continued to arise, so at this point Bush and Cheney entered the fray. Bush said: "we're at war...and in order to win the war, we must make sure the law enforcement men and women have got the tools necessary." Cheney, at a lunch with Republican senators, asked them to do their best to get the legislation passed through Congress by October 5.[52]

The rumors of biological attacks continued to spread over the next few days.[53] A front page article in *The New York Times* on September 30 was entitled, "Some Experts Say U.S. Is Vulnerable To a Germ Attack."[54] Anthrax was mentioned as a worry. In truth, anthrax letters were at that time already in circulation, but, according to the official account, no one but the perpetrators knew about them.

Indeed, on September 30 a major administration offensive began, with the aim of putting pressure on Congress to meet Cheney's new deadline of October 5. Among members of the executive branch stepping forward were Attorney General John Ashcroft, White House Chief of Staff Andrew Card, Secretary of Defense Donald Rumsfeld, and Secretary of Health and Human Services Tommy Thompson.[55] Ashcroft, appearing on CBS's Face the Nation, referred to the "likelihood of additional terrorist activity," and he made it clear that the terrorist activity could be expected to come from the same sources as the 9/11 attacks: "It's very unlikely that all of those associated with the attacks of Sept. 11 are now detained or have been detected." Card said that "terrorist organizations, like al Qaeda...have probably found the means to use biological or chemical warfare." Rumsfeld stated that terrorists could be equipped by their state sponsors with weapons of mass destruction. Tommy Thompson tried to strike a less distressing note, reassuring viewers on CBS's 60 Minutes, "that we're prepared to take care of any contingency, any consequence that develops for any kind of bioterrorism attack."

ABC's Peter Jennings, noting the difference in tone between apparent alarmists such as Card and those such as Thompson who sought to reassure the public, remarked (ABC News, October 1, 2001): "There's been some confusion for the public in the last 48 hours about whether the country should be worried about an attack using chemical or biological weapons." The program then went on to discuss the federal government's plans for how to deal with such attacks.

There was nothing subtle about the connection of all the speeches to the bill the administration wanted passed. The first line in the *Washington Post's* October 1 article on the topic was: "Bush administration officials said yesterday there will likely be more terrorist strikes in the United States, possibly including chemical and biological warfare, and they urged Congress to expand police powers by Friday [Oct. 5] to counter the threat."[56]

On the same day as this administration offensive, September 30, photo editor Robert Stevens, on vacation, came down with "flu-like symptoms" and crawled into the backseat of his car to rest, letting his wife take the wheel.[57] He had inhalation anthrax. His illness would be diagnosed on October 3 and he would die on October 5.

The press had carried articles throughout this period about biological attacks and anthrax. On September 28, for example, Rick Weiss of the *Washington Post* had written of the need to make an anthrax vaccine available to the public. Clinics across the country, he explained, were being swamped with requests for the vaccine.[58]

It is in this context that Leahy and Daschle's actions of October 2 must be understood. On that day it was determined that the administration's October 5 deadline would not be met. Both senators were directly implicated in the delay.

The *Washington Post* (October 3) gave the gist in the title of an important article on the subject: "Anti-terrorism Bill Hits Snag on the Hill; Dispute Between Senate Democrats, White House."[59] In the article we learn that, "Leahy accused the White House of reneging on an agreement." The issue was "a provision setting out rules under which law enforcement agencies could share wiretap and grand jury information with intelligence agencies." Leahy had been under the impression that his negotiations with the White House had produced an acceptable compromise; suddenly he discovered the compromise had been rejected. As Leahy balked, "Attorney General John D. Ashcroft accused the Democratic-controlled Senate of delaying legislation that he says is urgently needed to thwart another terrorist attack." The Senate, Ashcroft said "was not moving with sufficient speed." "Talk," he complained, "won't prevent terrorism," adding that he was "deeply concerned about the rather slow pace" at which the legislation was moving. Daschle, reports the article, supported Leahy. Although he was committed to seeing the legislation passed quickly, Daschle said that "he doubted the Senate could take up the legislation before next week." In other words, the October 5 deadline would not be met. Leahy and Daschle were the only Democratic senators mentioned in the article.

Although this small act of resistance may seem trivial to us today, Republican senator Orrin Hatch, supporting the administration, noted at the time: "It's a very dangerous thing."[60]

Apparently it was, indeed, a very dangerous thing. Shortly after the October 5 deadline passed with no enactment of the bill, letters containing anthrax spores were sent to Senators Leahy and Daschle. These letters were put in the mail sometime between October 6 and 9.[61]

It could be argued that mailing letters to the two senators was unnecessary since a compromise had been worked out on October 3-4.[62] But the executive was not seeking a compromise with this or that committee or with a few Democrats: it wanted the bill voted on and enacted without further delay. As it happened, the vote approving the bill in Senate did not take place until October 11, directly after the previously mentioned FBI warning. Even then, the legislation was not secure. The House and the Senate had passed different versions of the bill. The two had to be harmonized, and two separate votes needed to be held on the final version. Only then could Bush sign the final bill into law. The process did not come to a conclusion until October 26 and in the interim Congress would not be permitted to feel secure.

The dramatic action reached its high point with the opening of Daschle's letter. On October 15, *Roll Call*, a Washington newspaper dedicated to reporting news related to Capitol Hill, had as its front page headline: "HILL BRACES FOR ANTHRAX THREAT."[63] Sure enough, it was later that day that Grant Leslie, an intern working for Daschle, opened a letter to the senator to find two grams of spores of *B. anthracis* along with a text concluding with "ALLAH IS GREAT."[64] Due to the aerosolized ("floaty") nature of the anthrax spores, a characteristic not easy to achieve since in nature the spores tend to clump, many people in the Hart Senate building tested positive for exposure. There was general shock as it was discovered the spores, apparently treated in a sophisticated manner, had quickly contaminated the building.

The Hart Senate building had to be closed and the senators with offices there relocated. Much of the work by members of Congress to harmonize the two versions of the Patriot Act was carried out in unsettled conditions—in some cases in temporary quarters with limited computer access by senators writing on pads of paper.[65]

Once again the media concentrated on the anxiety produced: "A handful of anthrax particles sent through the mail to Senate Majority Leader Tom Daschle (D-S.D.) has sent Capitol Hill into an orbit of jitters and confusion..."[66]

Colbert King summed up the disturbance to Capitol Hill in an article in the *Washington Post* on October 27.[67] Noting that an aim of terrorism is "to instill feelings of fear and helplessness in citizens," he said:

> ...the perpetrators of the anthrax terror hit pay dirt in Washington. They've managed to accomplish what the British tried to generate with their burning of the White House, the Capitol and other government buildings in 1814—what Lee Harvey Oswald couldn't deliver in 1963—and what the Pentagon attackers sought to but couldn't provoke on Sept. 11: a sense of vulnerability and danger so great that it disables and fundamentally alters the way the nation's capital does its business.

"Anthrax," he added, "caused the House of Representatives to flee town; it closed Senate office buildings: unprecedented actions."

Finally, on October 26, Bush signed the bill into law. As he did so, he invoked the anthrax attacks as justification for the curtailment of civil rights:[68]

> The changes, effective today, will help counter a threat like no other nation has ever faced. We've seen the enemy, and the murder of thousands of innocent, unsuspecting people.
>
> They recognize no barrier of morality. They have no conscience. The terrorists cannot be reasoned with. Witness the recent anthrax attacks through our Postal Service.
>
> Our country is grateful for the courage the Postal Service has shown during these difficult times. We mourn the loss of the lives of Thomas Morris and Joseph Curseen; postal workers who died in the line of duty. And our prayers go to their loved ones...
>
> But one thing is for certain. These terrorists must be pursued, they must be defeated, and they must be brought to justice. And that is the purpose of this legislation.

Receipt of the anthrax letters did not fundamentally change the views of Daschle and Leahy. They had already given their support to the Patriot Act before they received their anthrax letters and they had committed themselves to getting the legislation passed quickly. On October 9 Daschle had said the legislation was "urgently needed" and that it ought to be passed "this week."[69] He made sure the bill went through. "At the urging of Senate Majority Leader Thomas A. Daschle (D-S.D.), [lawmakers] repeatedly turned aside efforts by Sen. Russell D. Feingold (D-Wis.) to amend the bill to address what he said were its failures to adequately protect civil liberties."[70]

When the bill was passed in the Senate shortly before midnight on October 11, Feingold stood alone against it.[71]

Leahy said, "Despite my misgivings, I have acquiesced in some of the administration's proposals because it is important to preserve national unity in this time of crisis."[72]

The attacks on the United States Congress were a central

part of the anthrax crimes. Congress members—intimidated, harassed, driven from their buildings, told not to wear their identification, and exposed to a deadly pathogen—gave in to the executive and acquiesced to its seizure of power.

If this assault on the legislative branch of government was, indeed, authored by members of the executive branch as an instance of the strategy of tension, the implications are enormous.

NSA Domestic Spying

As Congress was being pressured and intimidated, the executive did not wait for passage of the Patriot Act to begin spying on Americans. On December 20, 2013 U.S. federal officials publicly admitted for the first time that George W. Bush, on October 4, 2001, had "authorized sweeping collections of Americans' phone and Internet data."[73] On October 5, the NSA General Counsel had pronounced the program legal.[74] Thus began the NSA incursions on civil liberties that were to become well known.

On October 25, 2001 four members of Congress were briefed on the program, the rest of Congress being kept in the dark. The four initiates were Nancy Pelosi and Porter Goss, the Chair and Ranking Member of the House Permanent Select Committee on Intelligence; and Bob Graham and Richard Shelby, the Chair and Vice Chair of the Senate Select Committee on Intelligence.[75]

James Clapper, Director of National Intelligence, was the one who revealed the information about the October, 2001 initiation of the program. He later said that if American citizens had been asked to approve the domestic spying directly after 9/11 they probably would have done so. "I don't think it would be of any greater concern to most Americans than fingerprints."[76] The mistake, he felt, was in not being transparent. But, of course, there is no way of knowing what Americans would have approved if they had been asked. They had not been asked. Moreover, there is no reason to believe

Clapper would have made his information public at all if it had not been for a chain of events provoked by the Edward Snowden revelations.

At this time we can only speculate on the precise relationship of the NSA initiative to the anthrax attacks, but it is important to remember that there was a great deal more going on in the U.S. at this time than the trauma from September 11 mentioned in most accounts of NSA spying. There were almost daily warnings by the U.S. administration of further attacks to come; there were people taking Cipro, buying gas masks and attempting to get anthrax vaccines; and, as time went on, there were deaths from anthrax. On October 3, the day before Bush's signing of the order, Robert Stevens was diagnosed with anthrax. He died the day after the signing. Likewise, two days before the four members of Congress were briefed, two postal workers died of anthrax.

Later, defenders of the secret NSA program (the "Terrorist Surveillance Program") attempted to defend it as a legitimate interpretation of Section 215 of the Patriot Act. But this, of course, does not hold water. Bush signed the NSA order before the Patriot Act had been approved either by the Senate or by the House of Representatives.

Endnotes

1 Leonie Huddy, Nadia Khatib, and Theresa Capelos, "The Polls--Trends: Reaction to the Terrorist Attacks of September 11, 2001," *Public Opinion Quarterly* 66 (2002).

2 Tamar Lewin, "Anthrax Scare Prompts Run on an Antibiotic," *The New York Times*, September 27, 2001.

3 Serge Schmemann, "An Overview: Anthrax Anxiety at Home, Signs of Progress," *The New York Times*, October 16, 2001.

4 David Barstow, "Anthrax Found in NBC News Aide: Suspicious Letter Is Tested at Times--Wide Anxiety," *The New York Times*, October 13, 2001.

5 Jim Yardley, "The Anthrax Investigation: Anxiety Grows in South Florida as Mystery of Anthrax Cases Lingers," *The New York Times*, October 12, 2001.

6 R. W. Apple, "The Overview: As Anxiety Over Bioterrorism Grows, Bush Promises That the U.S. Will Stay Vigilant," *The New York Times*, October 14, 2001.

7 "Fears of Anthrax and Smallpox (Editorial)," *The New York Times*, October 7, 2001.
8 Ibid.
9 Ibid.
10 Ibid.
11 David Kocieniewski, "The Jitters: Nervousness Spreads, Though Illness Doesn't," *The New York Times*, October 11, 2001; Richard Jones, "Jitters: These Days, Even Soap Is a Suspicious Powder," *The New York Times*, October 18, 2001.
12 Kocieniewski, "The Jitters: Nervousness Spreads, Though Illness Doesn't."
13 Rick Weiss, "Source of Florida Anthrax Case Is Sought; Victim Dies as 50 Investigators Search," *The Washington Post*, October 6, 2001.
14 Darryl Fears, "Security Crackdown a Mixed Bag; Alert Varies From Calvert Cliffs to Disneyland, From Thorough to Easygoing," *Washington Post*, October 10, 2001.
15 Don Oldenburg, "Stocking Up in Hopes Of Breathing Easier; Gas Masks May Not Offer Protection," *The Washington Post*, October 10, 2001.
16 Michael Powell and Peter Slevin, "Detective, Scientists Exposed to Anthrax; FBI Continues to Hunt for Letters' Origins," *The Washington Post*, October 15, 2001.
17 Shankar Vendantam, "Bioterrorism's Relentless, Stealthy March; Confusion and Publicity Help to Heighten Public's Fear of Attack From Unknown," *The Washington Post*, October 18, 2001.
18 Dana Milbank, "Fear Is Here to Stay, So Let's Make The Most of It," *The Washington Post*, October 21, 2001.
19 "Terror Attacks The Mentally Ill," *The Washington Post*, October 23, 2001.
20 R. W. Apple, "City of Power, City of Fears," *The New York Times*, October 18, 2001; Michael Janofsky, "The False Alarms: Anthrax Fears Appear to Spread, Even Without New Verified Cases," *The New York Times*, October 17, 2001; Kocieniewski, "The Jitters: Nervousness Spreads, Though Illness Doesn't."
21 Daschle and D'Orso, *Like No Other Time: The 107th Congress and the Two Years That Changed America Forever*, 107 ff.
22 Ibid., 109.
23 Ibid., 110.
24 Ibid., 110 ff.
25 Ibid., 118.
26 Ibid., 117.
27 Morin, "Almost 90% Want U.S. To Retaliate, Poll Finds"; Huddy, Khatib, and Capelos, "The Polls--Trends: Reaction to the Terrorist Attacks of September 11, 2001."
28 Daschle and D'Orso, *Like No Other Time: The 107th Congress and the Two Years That Changed America Forever*, 125.
29 Susan Schmidt and Bob Woodward, "FBI, CIA Warn Congress of More Attacks As Blair Details Case Against Bin Laden; Retaliation Feared If

U.S. Strikes Afghanistan," *The Washington Post*, October 5, 2001.

30 David S. Broder and Eric Pianin, "U.S. Is Still Vulnerable To Attacks, Experts Say; Numerous 'Targets of Opportunity' Cited," *The Washington Post*, October 6, 2001.

31 Eric Pianin, "Ridge Assumes Security Post Amid Potential For New Attacks; FBI Warns Public, Private Entities To Observe 'Highest State of Alert,'" *The Washington Post*, October 9, 2001.

32 Spencer S. Hsu and Carol D. Leonnig, "Lawmakers Seek Ways To Secure U.S. Capitol; Temporary Street Closings; Pop-Up Barriers Considered," *The Washington Post*, October 10, 2001.

33 Sewell Chan and Carol D. Leonnig, "City Seeks More Aid For Terrorism Relief; Preparedness, Recovery Help Requested," *The Washington Post*, October 10, 2001.

34 David A. Fahrenthold and Carol D. Leonnig, "Police Bar Most Buses And Trucks Near Capitol; Sudden Security Move Surprises D.C. Officials," *The Washington Post*, October 11, 2001.

35 Dan Eggen and Bob Woodward, "Terrorist Attacks Imminent, FBI Warns; Bush Declared Al Qaeda Is 'On the Run'; Assaults on U.S. Called Possible in 'Next Several Days,'" *The Washington Post*, October 12, 2001.

36 David Griffin and Peter Scott, eds., *9/11 and American Empire: Intellectuals Speak Out*, vol. 1 (Olive Branch Press, 2006), 82. See also Daniele Ganser, "The 'Strategy of Tension' in the Cold War Period, *Journal of 9/11 Studies*, vol. 39, May 2014.http://www.journalof911studies.com/resources/2014GanserVol39May.pdf

37 "Congress of the United States: Senate Majority Leader," *The Free Dictionary: Legal Dictionary*, accessed May 22, 2014, http://legal-dictionary.thefreedictionary.com/Senate+Majority+Leader.

38 "How Congress Works: Rules of the Senate: Standing Committees," *United States Senate: Committee on Rules & Administration*, accessed May 22, 2014, http://www.rules.senate.gov/public/index.cfm?p=RuleXXV.

39 John Lancaster, "Anti-Terrorism Bill Is Approved; Bush Cheers House's Quick Action, but Civil Liberties Advocates Are Alarmed," *The Washington Post*, October 13, 2001.

40 Huddy, Khatib, and Capelos, "The Polls--Trends: Reaction to the Terrorist Attacks of September 11, 2001"; Kam Wong, "The Making of the USA PATRIOT Act II: Public Sentiments, Legislative Climate, Political Gamesmanship, Media Patriotism," *International Journal of the Sociology of Law* 34 (2006): 105–40.

41 "History Commons: US Civil Liberties: Patriot Act: April 25, 1996: New Anti-Terrorism Law Passed," n.d., http://www.historycommons.org/timeline.jsp?timeline=civilliberties&civilliberties_patriot_act=civilliberties_patriot_act.

42 John Ashcroft and Mueller, "Attorney General John Ashcroft Remarks: Press Briefing with FBI Director Robert Mueller" (FBI Headquarters, September 17, 2001), https://w2.eff.org/Privacy/Surveillance/Terrorism/20010917_ashcroft_mueller_statement.html.

43 Daschle and D'Orso, *Like No Other Time: The 107th Congress and the*

Two Years That Changed America Forever, 134.

44 Jonathan Krim and John Lancaster, "Ashcroft Presents Anti-Terrorism Plan to Congress; Lawmakers Promise Swift Action, Disagree on Extent of Measures," *The Washington Post*, September 20, 2001.

45 Ibid.

46 John Ashcroft, "Attorney General Remarks: Press Briefing" (FBI Headquarters, September 18, 2001), http://www.justice.gov/archive/ag/speeches/2001/0918pressbriefing.htm; John Ashcroft and Robert Mueller, "Attorney General Ashcroft and FBI Director Mueller Transcript: Media Availability with State and Local Law Enforcement Officials" (DOJ Conference Room, October 4, 2001), http://www.justice.gov/archive/ag/speeches/2001/agcrisisremarks10_4.htm; John Ashcroft, "Attorney General Ashcroft News Briefing," October 8, 2001, http://www.justice.gov/archive/ag/speeches/2001/agcrisisremarks10_08.htm.

47 Daschle and D'Orso, *Like No Other Time: The 107th Congress and the Two Years That Changed America Forever*, 135.

48 Walter Pincus, "Caution Is Urged on Terrorism Legislation; Measures Reviewed To Protect Liberties," *The Washington Post*, September 21, 2001.

49 "Transcript of President Bush's Address," *The Washington Post*, September 21, 2001.

50 Ellen Nakashima and Rick Weiss, "Biological Attack Concerns Spur Warnings: Restoration of Broken Public Health System Is Best Preparation, Experts Say," *The Washington Post*, September 22, 2001; editorial, "Taking Bio-Warfare Seriously," *The Washington Post*, September 23, 2001; Justin Blum and Dan Eggen, "Crop-Dusters Thought To Interest Suspects," *The Washington Post*, September 24, 2001; Rick Weiss et al, "Suspect May Have Wanted to Buy Plane; Inquiries Reported On Crop-Duster Loan," *The Washington Post*, September 25, 2001.

51 John Lancaster and Walter Pincus, "Proposed Anti-Terrorism Laws Draw Tough Questions; Lawmakers Express Concerns to Ashcroft, Other Justice Officials About Threat to Civil Liberties," *The Washington Post*, September 25, 2001.

52 John Lancaster, "Senators Question an Anti-Terrorism Proposal," *The Washington Post*, September 26, 2001.

53 John Anderson and Vernon Loeb, "Al Qaeda May Have Crude Chemical, Germ Capabilities," *The Washington Post*, September 27, 2001; Ceci Connolly, "Bioterrorism Vulnerability Cited; GAO Warns That Health Departments Are Ill-Equipped," *The Washington Post*, September 28, 2001; Rick Weiss, "Demand Growing for Anthrax Vaccine: Fear of Bioterrorism Attack Spurs Requests for Controversial Shot," *The Washington Post*, September 29, 2001;.

54 Sheryl Stolberg, "Some Experts Say U.S. Is Vulnerable To A Germ Attack," *The New York Times*, September 30, 2001.

55 Dana Milbank, "More Terrorism Likely, U.S. Warns; Bush Wants National Airport Reopened," *The Washington Post*, October 1, 2001. The Tommy Thompson quotation is taken from the author's own collection

of ABC News footage (Oct. 1, 2001), which includes Thompson's CBS performance.

56 Ibid.

57 Guillemin, *American Anthrax: Fear, Crime, and the Investigation of the Nation's Deadliest Bioterror Attack*, 18.

58 Weiss, "Demand Growing for Anthrax Vaccine: Fear of Bioterrorism Attack Spurs Requests for Controversial Shot.""

59 John Lancaster, "Anti-Terrorism Bill Hits Snag on the Hill; Dispute Between Senate Democrats, White House Threatens Committee Approval," *The Washington Post*, October 3, 2001.

60 Ibid.

61 "History Commons: 2001 Anthrax Attacks," October 6-9, 2001: Second Wave of Anthrax Attacks Targets Senators Daschle and Leahy.

62 John Lancaster, "Hill Is Due To Take Up Anti-Terror Legislation; Bill Prompts Worries Of Threat to Rights," *The Washington Post*, October 9, 2001.

63 John Bresnahan, "Hill Braces For Anthrax Threat," *Roll Call*, October 15, 2001.

64 Daschle and D'Orso, *Like No Other Time: The 107th Congress and the Two Years That Changed America Forever*, 147.

65 See, for example, Tish Schwartz, Chief Clerk/Administrator, House Committee on the Judiciary, "Effects of the Anthrax Attacks on the Drafting of the USA PATRIOT Act." History, Art & Archives, United States House of Representatives https://www.youtube.com/watch?v=M51REqSsy9A

66 Helen Dewar and Neely Tucker, "Tough Talk, Tears, Confusion and Concern," *The Washington Post*, October 18, 2001.

67 Colbert I. King, "Don't Give In to the Anthrax Scare," *The Washington Post*, October 27, 2001.

68 *President Bush Signs Anti-Terrorism Bill (text of Bush Remarks on Oct. 26, 2001 prior to His Signing of the USA PATRIOT Act)* (PBS Newshour, October 26, 2001), http://www.pbs.org/newshour/updates/terrorism/july-dec01/bush_terrorismbill.html?print.

69 Helen Dewar and Ellen Nakashima, "Airport Security Bill Still Mired in the Senate," *The Washington Post*, October 10, 2001.

70 John Lancaster, "Senate Passes Expansion of Electronic Surveillance; Anti-Terrorism Bill Is Set for House Debate Today," *The Washington Post*, October 12, 2001.

71 Ibid.

72 Ibid.

73 Ellen Nakashima, "US Reasserts Need to Keep Domestic Surveillance Secret," *Washington Post*, December 21, 2013.

74 "Timeline of NSA Domestic Spying," *Electronic Frontier Foundation*, accessed May 23, 2014, https://www.eff.org/nsa-spying/timeline.

75 Ibid.

76 Natasha Lennard, "Clapper: We Should Have Told You We Were Spying on You," *Salon*, February 18, 2014, http://www.salon.com/2014/02/18/clapper_we_should_have_told_you_we_were_spying_on_you/.

CHAPTER 5

PERPETRATOR HYPOTHESES

Who planned and carried out the anthrax attacks? In struggling with this question we should not rush too quickly to the discussion of individuals—Hatfill, Ivins, and the like—persons proposed by the FBI as lone-wolf perpetrators. A more useful approach is to sketch the possibilities in general terms and try to establish the actual historical movement of the investigation among them. Which possibilities were popular at particular moments? What arguments and evidence were offered in favor of them? By what path did the FBI arrive at its current preferred solution? Only when this overview is complete will we be ready to examine the FBI's ultimate choice of Dr. Bruce Ivins as "the anthrax killer."

The main perpetrator hypotheses can be arranged in four quadrants.

Quadrant 1: Foreign individual	Quadrant 2: Foreign group
Quadrant 3: Domestic individual	Quadrant 4: Domestic group

These four quadrants do not exhaust the possibilities, of course, because it is possible to imagine perpetrators from one quadrant working in association with perpetrators from another. We will return to this possibility at the end of this book.

The foreign individual hypothesis held little interest for anyone and, indeed, cannot explain basic facts about the attacks. There was never a serious attempt to promote it.

The domestic individual perpetrator was recognized as a possibility in the fall of 2001 (mention was made of a possible "domestic madman" along the lines of Ted Kaczynski, the so-called Unabomber[1]), but it had few supporters during the most intense phases of the attacks in October of 2001. It came to prominence only at the end of that month.

The main energy of the investigators and commentators was expended on promoting the foreign group hypothesis. Much evidence suggests that this option was meant to carry the day and was central to the original plan. An attack on the U.S. by groups of foreign Muslims using weapons of mass destruction could clearly serve to legitimize internal repression, external aggression, and a host of ancillary transformations. This scenario was established in advance of the anthrax attacks and pushed hard in October of 2001 as citizens got sick and died of anthrax, as the Patriot Act was pushed through Congress and the large scale NSA domestic spying was launched, as the invasion of Afghanistan began, and as preparations were made to invade Iraq.

Only when the sustainability of this preferred option was threatened was there a rapid shift to the domestic individual. This option was, the evidence suggests, chosen as the fallback position when exposure of the perpetrators and their accomplices became a danger. The FBI led the way to the domestic individual hypothesis, persisted with it, and remains committed to it to this day, despite its incompatibility with the evidence.

The hypothesis of the domestic group received minor

attention as the attacks began (we can find, for example, occasional references to the possibility that a neo-Nazi group was the perpetrator[2]) but after the FBI made its choice of the lone wolf, the domestic group became the suppressed possibility. Formally, the FBI kept this possibility alive,[3] but the Bureau worked hard to emphasize the search for an individual. One of the aims of the present book is to revitalize this suppressed hypothesis.

Let us now follow the movement between hypotheses in more detail.

Foreign Group

The narrative began in confusion but with two suspected foreign groups dominating media discourse: al-Qaeda and Iraq. As October progressed these two possibilities were increasingly seen as connected. The Double Perpetrator, involving both al-Qaeda and Iraq, although present in subtle form from the outset, entered the scene definitively in the middle of October and soon went from strength to strength.

The al-Qaeda Hypothesis

There were four main reasons the al-Qaeda hypothesis was attractive to many people.

(i) Al-Qaeda had been accused publicly by the President of the United States, and convicted in the media, of having carried out the 9/11 attacks. It seemed natural to many people that the same perpetrator would follow up with a second round of terrorist attacks.

Senator Tom Daschle says in his memoirs: "For weeks following September 11, there was a somewhat fatalistic expectation in the minds of many that we would be attacked again. The only question was where and how."[4] When he heard of Robert Stevens' death he thought this might be "round two."[5] He says that "the first thought most people had was that the letters were somehow connected to the September 11 attacks, that they were the work of a terrorist group such as al-Qaeda."[6]

As a matter of fact, already by mid-September the fear had been publicly expressed that biological attacks by al-Qaeda were in progress. On September 22 the *Washington Post* noted:[7]

> Soon after last week's terrorist attacks, federal health authorities told public health agencies to be on the alert for 'unusual disease patterns associated with today's events,' a bureaucratically phrased but nonetheless chilling hint of fear that the nation might be under biological attack.

The author of the article explicitly mentioned anthrax as a disease that could be unleashed on the population and expressed concern that the disease might not be diagnosed since it could "at first be mistaken as an ordinary cold or a flu." How odd that the anthrax attacks were, indeed, already in progress at this time. People started showing symptoms virtually on the day the article came out—symptoms that were, as the writer of the article had worried, not initially recognized as associated with anthrax.[8] As September wore on, the "anthrax scare" reached impressive proportions—Chapter 6 takes up the topic. All of this prescient commentary on anthrax assumed that the party that had carried out the 9/11 attacks, Bin Laden's group, would be the leading actor in any attack using anthrax.

(ii) United States forces began bombing Afghanistan on October 7. The Bush-Cheney administration claimed that, according to the best intelligence it was receiving, the U.S. population and the legislative branch should expect retaliation by al-Qaeda in a second serious round of terrorist attacks.

On October 5, two days before the bombing of Afghanistan began, "U.S. intelligence officials...told members of Congress there is a high probability that terrorists associated with Osama bin Laden will try to launch another major attack on American targets." An intelligence official claimed "there is a '100 percent' chance of an attack should the United States strike Afghanistan."[9]

(iii) Osama bin Laden and his group were said to be on record as expressing interest in acquiring biological weapons: these allegations were held to establish *intent*. Various spokespersons and authorities also said that al-Qaeda would have been able to develop at least a crude form of anthrax to use in an attack, and may have already developed it: these allegations were held to establish *capacity*. (See, for example, the September 27 *Washington Post* article, "Al Qaeda May Have Crude Chemical, Germ Capabilities."[10])

(iv) Circumstantial evidence, ranging from general to specific, strongly suggested a connection between the al-Qaeda operatives who were alleged to have carried out the 9/11 attacks (the Hijackers) and the anthrax attacks. The main types of evidence fall into four categories:

(a) Locations

The Hijackers had been active both in locations from which anthrax letters were sent and in places where people were exposed to the bacterium (especially in Florida). This was repeatedly noted by the FBI and the media.[11]

(b) Crop-duster planes

The Hijackers and other Middle Eastern men presumed to be associated with al-Qaeda had a close connection to crop-duster planes, which had been feared prior to 9/11 for their ability to disperse large quantities of biological and chemical weapons. These connections in 2000-2001 seemed firm and well established.[12]

(c) Links

There were curious apparent connections—some quite

direct—between anthrax and the Hijackers. Among these links was one of special importance that appeared to connect Robert Stevens, the first anthrax fatality, closely to several Hijackers, who were also in Florida.

(d) The letters

The text of the letters that accompanied several mailings of deadly spores had obviously been constructed to establish the perpetrators as extremist Muslims connected to the crimes of 9/11.

The first of these texts obtained by the FBI appears to have been that in the letter to journalist Tom Brokaw:[13]

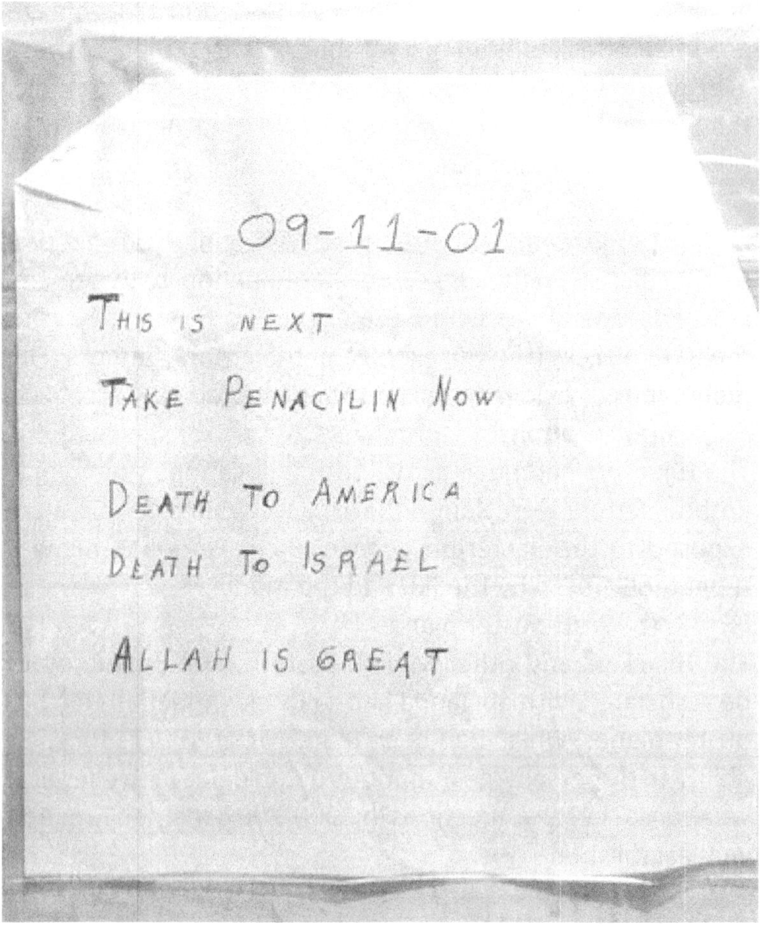
09-11-01

THIS IS NEXT

TAKE PENACILIN NOW

DEATH TO AMERICA

DEATH TO ISRAEL

ALLAH IS GREAT

The second distinct anthrax letter was that sent to Senator Tom Daschle:[14]

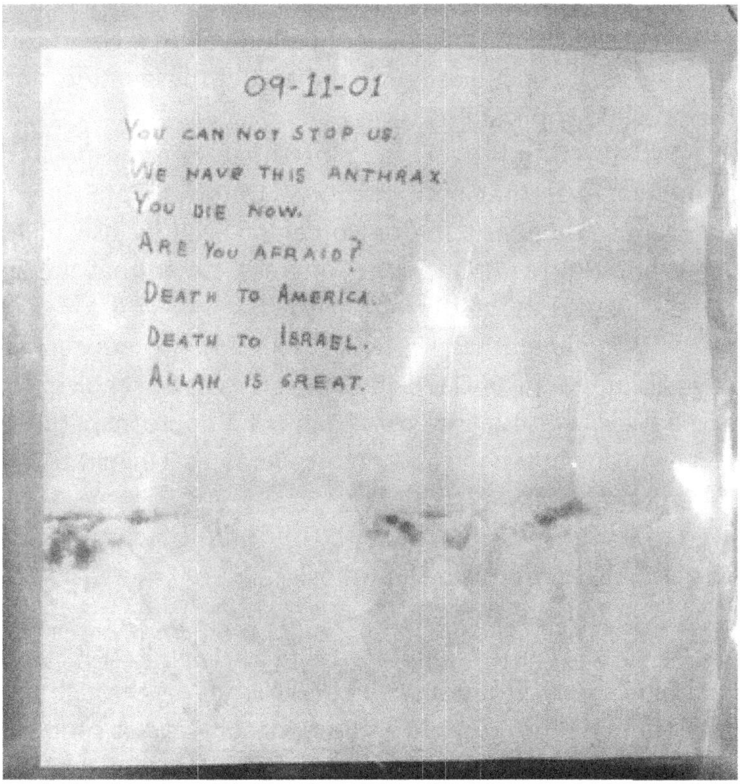
09-11-01

YOU CAN NOT STOP US.

WE HAVE THIS ANTHRAX.

YOU DIE NOW.

ARE YOU AFRAID?

DEATH TO AMERICA.

DEATH TO ISRAEL.

ALLAH IS GREAT.

The FBI obtained the Daschle letter on October 15, while it appears to have first read the Brokaw letter on October 12. Photographs of the above two letters, as well as of a letter to *The New York Post*, were first released to the public on October 23.[15]

The discovery of these letters, with their language of Muslim extremism and with the date "09-11-01" prominently displayed, helped create momentum toward the foreign group hypothesis and, specifically, toward al-Qaeda. On October 12 the FBI had been said by *The New York Times* to be "extremely doubtful" that the anthrax attacks were linked to the attacks of 9/11,[16] but on October 16 the same newspaper reported that investigators "abruptly acknowledged that such a link is now at the center of their investigation."[17] The al-Qaeda hypothesis now began to come into its own. Although the FBI never came out definitively in favor of this hypothesis, it could not ignore the text of these letters and the possible implications.

The cumulative effect of these arguments and suspicions was that by mid-to-late October, Tom Ridge, Assistant to the President for Homeland Security, as well as the White House and many in Congress, stated that the al-Qaeda hypothesis was the strongest.[18]

The general public, by October 21, also appears to have accepted the al-Qaeda hypothesis as its top choice: "In a *Newsweek* poll out yesterday [Oct. 21], 63 percent of those surveyed attributed the anthrax attacks at least in part to bin Laden's organization."[19]

The Double Perpetrator Hypothesis

What I call the "Double Perpetrator hypothesis" held that Bin Laden's group sent the anthrax spores through the mail but that the group had a state sponsor that had supplied the spores, namely Iraq.

The Double Perpetrator hypothesis had advantages over the simple al-Qaeda hypothesis. Spreading anthrax through mailed letters was a primitive and ineffective means of dispersing anthrax if the goal was multiple casualties. This crudity was reinforced by the text of the letters, with their misspellings and unidiomatic English. In the Double Perpetrator hypothesis these primitive elements could be laid at the feet of al-Qaeda, while the source of the sophisticated *B. anthracis* spores in the envelopes to the senators had to be a state, Iraq, which was known to have once possessed a stockpile of anthrax. A peculiar paradox was thus resolved.

The Double Perpetrator hypothesis, in its broad sense, was certainly not new. States can, and often do, support terrorist groups. For example, the United States sponsored terrorists in Nicaragua (the so-called "Contras") beginning in the late 1970s. In fact, in 1948 the CIA was explicitly given a mandate to support armed organizations subverting or attacking enemy states while ensuring that such support could be plausibly disclaimed by the U.S. government.[20] This relationship of sponsor-proxy is to be expected in the case of weapons of mass destruction, which are a scientific and financial challenge for non-state groups. In the Defense Against Weapons of Mass Destruction Act of 1996 the U.S. Congress recognized the danger of "extremist and terrorist movements, acting independently *or as proxies for foreign states*" (my emphasis). Through the sponsor-proxy relationship, the Act says, a foreign state is able to achieve "plausible deniability."[21]

Before the Double Perpetrator idea was promoted for the anthrax attacks it was applied to 9/11. Already on the day of 9/11 there were plenty of allusions to the possibility of a state sponsor of the attacks. The formal warning to state sponsors occurred at 8:30 p.m. on September 11 with Mr. Bush's words: "We will make no distinction between the terrorists who committed these acts and those who harbor them."[22]

A further expression of this idea was given in Bush's address to the Joint Session of the 107th Congress on September 20, 2001: "From this day forward, any nation that continues to harbor or support terrorism will be regarded by the United States as a hostile regime."[23]

What Bush said formally, many others said crudely. Neoconservative Charles Krauthammer explained on September 28 that the war against terrorism was not about chasing Osama bin Laden or other terrorists. The war was about getting rid of regimes. The message to be given to state sponsors of terrorism was: "Harbor terrorists—and your regime dies."[24] George Will said, some time later, that the choice to be given to state sponsors of terrorism was "reform or extinction."[25] Both spoke openly about Iraq as a target.

What had occurred in relation to 9/11 soon occurred for the anthrax attacks. Already in their surprisingly timely book, *Germs: Biological Weapons and America's Secret War*, published in early October of 2001, Judith Miller and co-authors William Broad and Stephen Engelberg explained that Iraq might use a "surrogate, a terrorist group" to deliver a bioweapon to its target.[26] This scenario had also been incorporated into the June, 2001 bioterrorism exercise called Dark Winter, carried out at Andrews Air Force Base, about which more will be said in Chapter 6. Likewise, Iraq's role as a potential supplier of anthrax spores was discussed in the press while the attacks were actually occurring but before they were publicly known. For example, on September 27, a microbiologist at the Monterey Institute of International Studies said, in the course of an interview about the dangers of bioweapons, that al-Qaeda "could also conceivably obtain a virulent strain of anthrax from Iraq."[27]

James Woolsey, Director of Central Intelligence under Clinton, had begun associating Iraq with the 9/11 attacks on September 11 itself (shortly after 7 p.m., ET),[28] and as the anthrax attacks unfolded he added these to Iraq's sins.[29]

The story of Mohamed Atta, alleged ringleader of the Hijackers, meeting with Iraqi intelligence in Prague in April of 2001 (discussed later in this chapter), was of great assistance in establishing the crucial links between Iraq and al-Qaeda, promoting the Double Perpetrator idea for both sets of fall attacks.

Citing credible and substantive evidence of Iraqi links to the anthrax attacks was generally not thought to be necessary by those making these accusations, but insinuation was common. On October 18, for example, journalist Richard Cohen wrote in the *Washington Post* that, "Saddam and his bloody bugs have to go." Cohen admitted that Iraq might not have had anything to do with the anthrax attacks, but since "America is now getting a taste of the havoc biological weapons can wreak," and since "Iraq has such a capacity,"

Iraq must be placed in the crosshairs.[30] Robert Kagan, leading neo-conservative and one of the founders of the Project for the New American Century, wrote on October 17 that if George H. W. Bush had toppled Saddam's government in 1991, "today we wouldn't all be wondering whether anthrax spores spreading around the country were developed in one of Saddam's laboratories."[31]

Through October of 2001, accusations against Iraq grew and became more specific. On October 14 *The Observer* in the U.K. reported:[32]

> American investigators probing anthrax outbreaks in Florida and New York believe they have all the hallmarks of a terrorist attack—and have named Iraq as prime suspect as the source of the deadly spores. Their inquiries are adding to what US hawks say is a growing mass of evidence that Saddam Hussein was involved, possibly indirectly, with the September 11 hijackers.

The article continued:

> Leading US intelligence sources, involved with both the CIA and the Defence Department, told *The Observer* that the 'giveaway' which suggests a state sponsor for the anthrax cases is that the victims in Florida were afflicted with the airborne form of the disease.

The Observer also quoted an anonymous CIA source as saying, "they aren't making this stuff in caves in Afghanistan." The source continued: "This is prima facie evidence of the involvement of a state intelligence agency. Maybe Iran has the capability. But it doesn't look likely politically. That leaves Iraq."

On October 15 the *Wall Street Journal* spoke approvingly of *The Observer's* report, noting, "Bin Laden couldn't be doing all this in Afghan caves. The leading supplier suspect has to be Iraq." The *Wall Street Journal* also had a course of action to recommend: "The best defense against anthrax attacks...is to go on relentless offence."[33] The alleged Prague meeting between an Iraqi diplomat and Mohamed Atta was mentioned in the same piece, with the result that Iraq was now a definite target.

The reporters for *The Observer* noted that preparations for bombing Iraq were already underway and they named the individuals at the center of this effort: "The hawks winning the ear of President Bush is [*sic*] assembled around Defense Secretary Donald Rumsfeld, his deputy Paul Wolfowitz, and a think tank, the Defense Policy Advisory Board, dubbed the 'Wolfowitz cabal.'"

The Observer's story seems a bit premature: it would have been better founded a few days later when the sophisticated, aerosolized Daschle anthrax had been studied. (The FBI did not receive the highly sophisticated spores in the Daschle letter until October 15.) In any case, the motif "they aren't making this stuff in caves" definitely preceded evidence justifying it. The motif seems to have made its first appearance in the *Washington Post* on October 5 in an article by Charles Krauthammer. When Krauthammer wrote the article—assuming he wrote it on October 4—Robert Stevens had been diagnosed with anthrax (this was announced in a press conference on October 4) but was still alive. Although he was known to have the inhalation form of the disease, little of significance was known about the spores, where he had contracted the disease, and whether his disease was the result of an attack or was simply acquired from the environment. What is more, Krauthammer did not even mention Stevens or his disease in the article. Nonetheless, after ranting about biological attacks and the importance of going after enemy states with weapons of mass destruction, he observed: "You do not make weaponized anthrax in caves. For that you need serious scientists and serious laboratories, like the ones in Baghdad."[34] The comment was bizarre. There was no credible evidence of "weaponized" anthrax anywhere on the scene when he wrote the article.

After October 15, discussions of "weaponized anthrax," grounded in study of the attack spores, became increasingly common. An attempt was made to use the physical characteristics of the anthrax spores to establish Iraq as the source of the spores. But it was a risky move and it ultimately backfired, discrediting both foreign group hypotheses and almost exposing the perpetrators.

The Fall of the Double Perpetrator Hypothesis

The perpetrators of the anthrax attacks, in attempting to set up al-Qaeda and Iraq as the Double Perpetrator, made several mistakes.

The first mistake had to do with the type of anthrax used in all of the letters, the Ames strain. (A "strain" is a genetic subtype of a bacterium.) Originally isolated from a cow in Texas—called the Ames strain because it was mistakenly thought to have originated in Ames, Iowa—this type of anthrax was more common in U.S. labs than elsewhere. It was central to U.S. military work on anthrax and it certainly did not point in the direction of al-Qaeda or Iraq. But how could the perpetrators have been so ill-advised as to use this strain when they could, presumably, have used others more likely to implicate Iraq?

It was widely believed, even by microbiologists well acquainted with anthrax, that the Ames strain had become so broadly dispersed throughout laboratories across the world that this identification would not say much about the origin of the samples in the letters—or otherwise put, could easily be used to implicate Iraq. The perpetrators may have shared this misconception.[35]

Eventually, the FBI drew up a detailed list of laboratories around the world that were known to have the Ames strain: neither Iraq nor al-Qaeda was on that list. According to the Bureau, only 15 U.S. laboratories and three foreign labs possessed the Ames strain.[36]

Another possible reason for use of the Ames strain by the perpetrators was that they intended from the outset to frame one or more persons within the U.S. microbiology community. If such parties could have been credibly connected to the Ames strain and portrayed as acting on behalf of Iraq, they would have been good candidates for framing. Ayaad Assaad, a scientist who apparently had been subjected to racial harassment while working for the United States Army Medical Research Institute of Infectious Diseases (USAMRIID), could have been that candidate.[37] He had worked for USAMRIID until 1997. On October 2, 2001 the FBI received a letter (postmarked on September 26) calling Assaad "a potential biological terrorist." It is difficult to believe that this was a coincidence given that the attacks were underway but not yet made public.

The FBI interviewed Assaad on October 3 but decided for reasons unknown to us not to follow this lead.

Another mistake made by the perpetrators had to do with the weaponization of the attack spores. By the time the perpetrators targeted the two U.S. senators they were employing extremely sophisticated anthrax spores. It was clear that this was exceptionally lethal material that had undergone considerable modification from its natural state. The spores dispersed quickly and widely, threatening far more lives than would anthrax spores in their natural state. Tom Daschle has remarked on this feature of the spores in his memoirs:[38] "The researchers were stunned to confirm not only the high aerosolizability of this anthrax, but its ability to reaerosolize so readily a month after the original spill." He has also confirmed that scientists at USAMRIID who studied the elusive, aerosolized material "had trouble keeping it under the microscope long enough to examine it."

Over the course of October, 2001 the media reported

that the anthrax spores were small and quite uniform in size, and this range (1.5-3 microns) was ideal if the spores were to enter the lungs and lodge there. Moreover, the spores appeared to have been treated with an additive that neutralized the electrostatic charge that, in nature, makes anthrax spores cling to each other and form clumps. Preventing the formation of clumps is essential to the process of aerosolization.[39]

As October, 2001 neared its end a struggle appeared to be taking place among members of the executive branch. It is possible this was staged, but evidence suggests this was a genuine conflict, with one party determined to keep following the original plan of framing the Double Perpetrator while the other party was equally determined to beat a strategic retreat into the haunts of the domestic lone wolf.

The claims and counterclaims in the *Washington Post* tell the story. On October 24 and 25 the tension was building. The FBI was now reported as saying privately that it suspected the source of the spores was domestic.[40] The White House, as well as many in Congress, was said to still lean toward al-Qaeda,[41] but it was obvious the proponents of the domestic perpetrator hypothesis were growing more outspoken. Meanwhile, the White House was said to be backing off its accusations against Iraq.[42] But this retreat from Iraqi provenance caused its own difficulties because the anthrax, being sophisticated, could not have been produced by al-Qaeda.

The discovery that there was an aerosolizing additive in the spores, announced on October 25, brought matters to a head.[43] Only three countries in the world were now said to have the capability of producing this anthrax: the former Soviet Union, the United States, and Iraq. While this opened up an opportunity for the get-Iraq group, it also had grave risks. Some experts were already saying that the U.S. was the leading contender as producer of these spore preparations.[44]

Suddenly, the White House began retreating not only from the Iraq hypothesis but also from the al-Qaeda hypothesis. Ari Fleischer, making an about-face, said on October 26 that, in the words of the *Washington Post*, "a skilled microbiologist and a small sophisticated lab would be capable of producing" the Daschle anthrax.[45]

Readers of the *Washington Post* were now told a disagreement had developed between the Bush administration and a separate party, of which James Woolsey was a representative, that wanted Iraq to remain the chief suspect as source of the spores.

Those favoring the domestic option, although they were said to be speaking "on condition of anonymity," were at least speaking, and the strength of their voices grew daily.[46] But the party promoting Iraq's involvement did not give up easily. Anthrax expert Richard Spertzel had explained on October 25 that Iraq used "aluminum-based clays or silica powders" as additives to its anthrax spores[47] and the very next day ABC News entered the fray with the claim that the spores showed evidence of precisely these clays.

Brian Ross was the lead journalist. He reported that "sources tell ABCNEWS the anthrax in the tainted letter sent to Senate Leader Tom Daschle was laced with bentonite. The potent additive is known to have been used by only one country in producing biochemical weapons—Iraq." This shocking information had been relayed to ABC, supposedly, by "three well-placed and separate sources."[48] ABC continued to repeat this claim and by October 29 its "well-placed and separate sources" had grown to four.[49] In addition, ABC added to this article a detailed version of the tale of Atta in Prague. The bentonite story and the Prague story were obviously meant to reinforce each other, and Iraq was the target.

But the bentonite did not exist. On November 1, Ross was forced to inform his audience that further tests had ruled out bentonite.[50] Significantly, it was the White House that contradicted Ross's bentonite claim and that appears to have made him back down.[51] The takeaway is that Ross's sources—and this applies as well to one of his 2002 tales discussed in the next chapter—remained determined to frame Iraq even after the White House had been persuaded to give it up and was moving on to the lone wolf theory.

Journalist Glenn Greenwald has castigated ABC for its false claims, saying in 2008 that "the role played by ABC News in this episode is the single greatest, unresolved media scandal of this decade."[52]He has also said it was likely that "the same people responsible for perpetrating the attacks were the ones who fed the false reports to the public, through ABC News, that Saddam was behind them."

But ABC News had actually brought into further disrepute the framing of Iraq, and by this time it had become clear that in using such a sophisticated and lethal preparation of spores the perpetrators had crawled out on a limb. They had, in effect, ruled out the hypothesis that al-Qaeda, acting alone, had carried out the attacks. Al-Qaeda, in its famed caves, could not possibly have created this product, and now the Iraqi provenance was cashiered as well.

Ultimately, the failure to successfully frame Iraq as source of the spores not only ruined the hypothesis of al-Qaeda acting alone but also ruined what might otherwise have been credible domestic hypotheses: the right-wing hate group and the eccentric loner. Neither could have created this product.

A final major mistake the perpetrators made was the crude forging of letters from Muslim extremists. Although the FBI initially seemed to be moving, after reading the Daschle letter, in the direction of al-Qaeda, the Bureau soon turned in the opposite direction. The letters were an embarrassment. It was as if someone had tried to frame Native Americans for the crime by inserting a note in the letters announcing, "White man in heap big trouble."

On October 24 members of the FBI were saying privately to the media that they doubted the links to al-Qaeda were real and believed there was a U.S. source of the spores. While the White House was still supporting the al-Qaeda hypothesis, the *Washington Post* reported that "many experts believe the phrases [in the letters] are intended to wrongly cast suspicion on foreign terrorists."[53] The *Washington Post* also reported that "Retired Air Force anti-terrorism specialist Gerald 'Gary' Brown said he doubts the anthrax attacks are the work of Muslims." "We believe this is home grown," said Brown.[54] Other experts added, "It's what every American thinks a Muslim fanatic would write."

In short, the anthrax letters, taken as a combined production of text and spores, failed to support either the al-Qaeda or the Double Perpetrator hypotheses. The text was not believably al-Qaeda and the spores were not believably Iraqi.

From about the end of October, 2001, although the get-Iraq group fought a rear-guard action, the anthrax attacks were increasingly accepted as a domestic operation. The foreign group hypothesis was on the ropes.

Journalistic Fictions Fan the Flames

Throughout September and October of 2001 those outraged by the attacks of the purported Double Perpetrator ranted against scenarios conjured up by their own imaginations.

On October 21 the *Washington Post* published a review by Jeff Stein of the book *Germs*, by Judith Miller and co-authors.[55] Stein pointed out that it is not easy to master the art of bioweapons production and commented:

> That should give some comfort to Americans terrified by the prospect of an imminent biological or chemical attack by Osama Bin Laden's operatives within our borders. But it probably won't, especially considering that

> Bin Laden's evil pal Saddam Hussein perfected the weapons—and used them—against Iranian troops and Kurdish villagers...

The warm relationship between the Islamist Bin Laden and the secular-nationalist Saddam was fantasy, of course. But Stein was not finished. He continued:

> And once again, we've sent a stern warning to Saddam Hussein that Iraq will catch fire if weapons of mass destruction are unleashed here. He should know that few Americans, in their present angry and anxious mood, can imagine weeping much if Baghdad is nuked while millions here are dying from smallpox.

The millions of Americans dying of smallpox were a fictional projection, taken equally from the Miller book and from the Dark Winter simulation. Yet the *Post* gave Stein free rein to fantasize about a retaliatory nuclear strike against a city inhabited by several million human beings. We might be tempted to dismiss all this as a bad joke, but we do not have that luxury: the theme of using nuclear weapons against fantasized Muslim attackers was also taken up by others and is a sign of a dangerous orientation that remains with us to this day. (See chapter 8.)

The day after the Stein article the *Washington Post* published a similar article by Fred Hiatt.[56]

> A hit squad from somewhere in the Middle East travels to New York City carrying a one-liter bottle filled with one of the several chemical weapons agents we have long known Saddam Hussein to be developing. Using a simple sprayer (like one that a gardener or house painter might own), they diffuse the contents into the air over Times Square...

> Hundreds, maybe thousands of people die agonizing deaths as a result.

And on it goes. Fiction again—in this case taken from a book by former UN weapons inspector Richard Butler. Hiatt, while admitting the scenario was fictional and that there was no actual evidence to tie Iraq to the anthrax attacks, insisted that Saddam Hussein was a "plausible suspect." He told his readers that Saddam was "credibly alleged to have tested germ weapons on prison inmates" (there has never been any evidence to support this allegation), and ended by saying that it would be a pity if Americans, faced with the prospect of a dangerous Iraq, exhibited "faintheartedness."

In short, once again Americans were projected as dying in large numbers from Iraq's weapons of mass destruction on the pages of the *Washington Post*, and once again Iraq was to be held accountable, even though those dead Americans, like Iraq's weapons of mass destruction, were products of the imagination.

But the widest circulation was achieved by the tale, Mohamed Atta Visits Prague.[57] This story was apparently first told by the Associated Press on September 18, 2001. It concerned a meeting of Mohamed Atta, alleged ringleader of the Hijackers, with an Iraqi intelligence agent. They supposedly met in Prague in April of 2001. Through the fall of 2001 the story was retold with an astonishing amount of detail as well as confirmation by Czech intelligence. It was widely circulated, and into the winter of 2001-02 was still endorsed by Colin Powell and Dick Cheney. While many people remember that the tale functioned to link Iraq to the 9/11 attacks, it should not be forgotten that the story also functioned to link Iraq to the anthrax attacks. At times the link was implied directly:

> Some federal officials have wondered whether chemical or biological weapons might have

> been a subject of discussion when Mohamed Atta, one of the Sept. 11 hijackers, met last year with an Iraqi intelligence official in Prague. Iraq is known to have worked on the development of such weapons.[58]

More generally, bearing in mind that in October 2001 there was a strenuous effort to associate the Hijackers with the anthrax attacks, we can understand that Mohamed Atta Visits Prague was being used to make several linkages. It linked al-Qaeda, 9/11, anthrax and Iraq.

The story was fiction.[59] Atta did not meet with Iraqi intelligence in Prague. This was confirmed progressively in the media from spring to fall, 2002.

The FBI's Case and Its Failure

By the end of October 2001, the main lines of the subsequent FBI account were beginning to emerge. The FBI would direct the search party away from evil Muslims—both al-Qaeda and Iraq—and would quietly, over a period of years, pursue the domestic lone wolf perpetrator. Although this story would be of doubtful value to the executive's foreign policy ambitions it would have the virtue of disguising the real purpose of the anthrax attacks and burying the issue of who was behind them.

On August 6, 2002 Attorney General John Ashcroft named scientist Steven Hatfill a "person of interest" and the FBI concentrated on investigating him, publicly and aggressively. A year later Hatfill sued the Justice Department for libel, and eventually he received $5.82 million in compensation, while the FBI moved on to other possibilities.[60]

In 2008 the Bureau decided the "anthrax killer" was Dr. Bruce Ivins, who had been working on an anthrax vaccine at the U.S. Army Medical Research Institute of Infectious Diseases (USAMRIID) at Fort Detrick in Maryland. This time the FBI faced no serious challenge from its chosen perpetrator because Ivins died shortly before he was to be charged with the crime. He was said to have committed suicide.[61] If he took his life—a likelihood given his mental instability and the extent of FBI harassment and pressure—the FBI must bear some responsibility.

In 2010 the Department of Justice (DOJ) formally closed the case, affirming Ivins' guilt.[62]

But the case against Ivins was subjected to serious critique from the beginning. On October 2, 2009, attorney Barry Kissin, responding to an invitation by one of Congressman Rush Holt's aides, submitted a detailed and historically important memo to Mr. Holt's office on the anthrax attacks and the associated cover-up.[63]

In his submission Kissin showed that the anthrax spores, clearly from a domestic source, had been subjected to sophisticated processes that would have been impossible for a lone wolf perpetrator to perform. He pointed out that the domestic U.S. anthrax program had gone underground when Nixon ordered destruction of biological weapons materials in 1969 but that during the late 1990s the CIA was directly involved in the development of both weaponized anthrax and the means of delivering it as a weapon. Because of these clandestine programs, he argued, the U.S. military-industrial complex possessed, prior to the anthrax attacks, all the elements essential for the attacks. These elements included: the Ames strain of anthrax; methods of refining the spores to achieve the right size and uniformity for maximum lethality; and a method of promoting dispersibility through the addition of silicon to the spores. Kissin referred as well to domestic studies relevant to sending the attack spores through the mail:

> In 1999, William Patrick, the original inventor of anthrax weaponization, was commissioned to do an analysis of a hypothetical anthrax

> attack through the mail for the CIA. Ultimately, this classified document was leaked to the media. In his report entitled "Risk Assessment," Patrick explained that 2.5 grams is the amount that can be placed into a standard envelope without detection. (The anthrax letters addressed to the Senators contained about 2 grams of anthrax.) In a footnote, Patrick noted that the U.S. had refined "weaponized" anthrax powder to the unprecedented extent of a trillion spores per gram. This degree of refinement corresponds with the extraordinary purity of the anthrax in the letters addressed to the Senators.

Kissin argued that one of the chief suspects in the attacks ought to be Battelle Memorial Institute, the largest R&D company in the world, which regularly does work for the CIA and the U.S. military and was involved in anthrax weaponization projects that began in the second half of the 1990s. He noted that Battelle had the facilities for working with dry anthrax spores, while USAMRIID did not. Battelle publicizes its advanced methods of producing a variety of sophisticated aerosols. Kissin also showed how, throughout the anthrax investigation, the FBI had taken steps to keep Battelle's name out of the discussion.

Kissin dismissed the FBI's attempt to explain the silicon in the attack anthrax, the substantial presence of which was not in doubt, as "naturally" occurring. Experiments had demonstrated that the deliberate addition of silicon is the only way to explain the high amounts of this chemical element in the anthrax. Silicon has long been key to American methods of weaponizing anthrax.

Kissin likewise rejected the FBI's attempt to claim that the silicon in the attack spores was innocent because it was located in the spore coat rather than in the outermost layer, the exosporium. The FBI, he argued, was concealing the fact that the original anthrax weaponization technology, which involved situating the silicon in the exosporium, had been surpassed by technology of microencapsulation that situates silicon in the underlying spore coat.

If the FBI's case was vulnerable to this powerful critique in 2009, the trouble has only increased since then. Since 2011, a scientific report, a court case, a set of research articles, and several other sorts of evidence have further discredited FBI contentions.

The National Academy of Sciences Report

In 2008 the FBI asked the National Academy of Sciences (NAS) to carry out a review of the scientific methods used by the Bureau in the course of its anthrax investigation. There is no reason to believe the FBI was ever keen on this option. FBI Director Robert Mueller had been subjected to tough Congressional questioning after Ivins' death in 2008 and had chosen the NAS option to avoid a more comprehensive investigation.[64]

The NAS project, carried out by a committee consisting initially of 15 scientists, started its work in 2009 and submitted its final report in 2011.[65] The committee had constraints and it also had to suffer through what appear to have been internal conflicts within the DOJ and FBI.

The committee's job was not to examine anthrax spores, or equipment that might have been used to prepare the anthrax, or any other physical evidence. The committee was restricted to reviewing reports, studies and papers produced by others, as well as interviewing a number of witnesses. The NAS committee had no mandate to evaluate the broad forensic study that had led to the finding of Ivins as the killer, nor did it have a mandate to comment on the overall strength of the case against Ivins.

Although the committee politely expresses, in its

report, appreciation of the FBI and its hard work, a careful reading reveals a more complex picture.[66] For example:

- The committee received two large boxes with approximately 9000 pages of material that it was asked to review, but the FBI did not provide a clear explanation of the material or a system of consistent coding, so a great deal of time was spent organizing the material and trying to determine its significance.
- The committee found out late in the game that there was a body of classified material bearing on the investigation to which it would not have access.
- The committee asked the FBI several times for a written statement of the conclusions the FBI drew from its scientific investigations, but no such statement was ever forthcoming.
- FBI members interviewed by the committee tried to formulate the FBI's goals and conclusions but these were not consistent with each other or with written statements from the DOJ.
- FBI members were sometimes helpful but at other times were terse and unhelpful.

In addition, the FBI dumped a new set of documents on the NAS committee after the committee had submitted its draft report. Since there was no reason the FBI could not have given this material much earlier, the move generated much criticism. Congressman Rush Holt suggested the dumping of new documents may have been an attempt "to contest and challenge the independent NAS panel's draft findings."[67]

It is difficult not to conclude that while one segment of the DOJ and FBI may have been willing to see the Bureau's anthrax work scrutinized, another segment definitely was not. This apparent conflict has surfaced from time to time in the FBI's anthrax investigation.

The NAS committee's final report, appearing in 2011,

was entitled *Review of the Scientific Approaches Used During the FBI's Investigation of the 2001 Anthrax Letters*. Well before publication it became known that the committee was finding serious flaws in the Bureau's case against Ivins, and this appears to be why the DOJ, or elements within it, took two sets of actions to counter the report.

First, the DOJ made a pre-emptive strike on the committee by definitively pronouncing Ivins the killer and closing the case before the committee's final report was published.[68]

Then, when the committee released its report and made its findings public, gaining considerable media attention, the FBI was quick to state that it had full confidence in its case against Ivins, and that the committee touched on only certain aspects of the physical evidence whereas the FBI's case was complex and was built on many forms of evidence. The Bureau then, through various intermediaries, had a "panel of experts" convened to review Ivins' psychiatric file.[69] This panel duly supported the FBI's conclusion that he was the anthrax killer. Unfortunately for the FBI, the panel was largely bogus and its report appears to have had little influence.[70]

Two of the NAS committee's findings severely weakened the FBI's case against Ivins.

The FBI had claimed that Ivins, when asked to submit a sample of the anthrax in his flask (the so-called RMR-1029 anthrax) to the FBI for its anthrax repository, falsified his submission.[71] This made Ivins appear deceptive and suspect. The NAS committee, however, did not find the evidence of deception compelling.[72]

Second, and more importantly, the committee severed the physical link between Ivins and the anthrax used in the mailings. To appreciate the importance of this it is crucial to understand that the case against Ivins was never strong. The characterization of the case in *The New York Times* as "circumstantial" is generous.[73] The most important piece of evidence presented had to do with the spores used in the mailings. FBI scientists claimed they could trace the deadly spores to a flask of liquid anthrax preparation, called RMR-1029, kept under Ivins' care in his lab. The FBI did not claim that the spores in the letters had been directly taken from Ivins' flask, rather they said that the anthrax in Ivins' flask was the material from which the spores in the mailings had been derived. In other words, the FBI claimed someone had taken material from the flask and grown colonies of anthrax from it. Anthrax from these colonies, or from descendants of these colonies, had then been used in the deadly mailings. According to the FBI, "By 2007, investigators conclusively determined that a single spore-batch created and maintained by Dr. Bruce Ivins at USAMRIID was the parent material for the letter spores."[74] This, said the Bureau, pointed directly to Ivins as the killer.

Actually, even if this claim about RMR-1029 had been justified, the case against Ivins would have remained weak. Many people, both at USAMRIID and elsewhere, had access to anthrax deriving from the beaker in question. As Ivins' lawyer, Paul Kemp, pointed out in 2010, "there are dozens, if not hundreds, of scientists, contractors, students, professors, who used that same anthrax, the very anthrax that would have the same genetic components as RMR-1029."[75] It is difficult to see how a court case based on such evidence could have been successful.

But the NAS committee's findings dramatically weakened an already weak case. The committee found that the method used by FBI scientists was inadequate to support the conclusions drawn. The committee said the anthrax in the mailings could have derived from what was in Ivins flask, after one or more intermediate stages of culturing, *but the anthrax spores in the mailings could have come from a different source altogether*. The committee said the evidence was simply inconclusive.[76]

The NAS committee thus removed the main pillar in the case against Ivins.

The Stevens Court Case

The family of the first person to die in the anthrax attacks, Robert Stevens, took the U.S. government to court in 2003.[77] By this time it was widely accepted that the foreign group hypotheses about the anthrax had failed and that the anthrax had come from a U.S. laboratory, probably at USAMRIID, or at Dugway Proving Ground in Utah, or at Battelle Memorial Institute in Ohio. The plaintiff's case was built on allegations of negligence by the U.S. government, which, it claimed, had created conditions that allowed for the removal of deadly anthrax from one of these institutions. The lawyers for the Stevens family claimed that the U.S. government should have been aware of how deadly the anthrax was and should have put in place proper measures to insure it would not be removed by anyone bent on committing a crime with a bioweapon. Stevens' family sued for $50 million.

The U.S. government defense was conducted by a team of lawyers from the civil division of the Department of Justice. The February, 2010 "Amerithrax" report claiming that Ivins was the anthrax killer had been produced by the criminal division.

Since the lawyers for the civil division were defending the U.S. government against negligence, the FBI's story about Ivins was presumably seen by them as contrary to the interests they had to defend. If Ivins did, in fact, successfully smuggle anthrax from USAMRIID after preparing it in a lab there, the Stevens family would be right in its claim—this would, indeed, indicate negligence on the part of the U.S. government. Fortunately for the legal team, there was plenty of evidence available, including that from the NAS investigation, that cast doubt on the Ivins story. The team made use of this evidence.

The key document in this connection is titled, "Defendant United States' Motion for Summary Judgment

Based on the Absence of Proximate Cause and Memorandum of Law in Support." The text of this argument is 21 pages long and is publicly available. It was filed on July 15, 2011 in Florida Southern District.[78]

A "summary judgment" is a legal judgment made without a full trial. The DOJ legal team was asking the judge to make a judgment against the plaintiff because the plaintiff's lawyers had failed to provide evidence of a direct cause of the injury in question. The basic argument made by the DOJ legal team was that a plaintiff cannot simply rely upon a vague or indirect causal relationship. If A (in this case the U.S. government) is to be held responsible for B's injury (the death of Robert Stevens) B or B's representative must show that A acted in a particular way that had a specific, direct and foreseeable effect on B's welfare.

The DOJ civil lawyers did not say in this July submission that Ivins was not responsible for the anthrax crime but neither did they say that he was, even though the DOJ had closed the case the previous year and pronounced Ivins the anthrax killer in no uncertain terms. The civil team's argument was based on demonstrating the absence of evident connection between Ivins' flask and the attack anthrax.

A key point made by the civil legal team was that the anthrax in the mailings was "weaponized:" the attacks constituted a bioweapon attack on U.S. citizens. Although this may seem obvious, the FBI had strenuously denied it during most of its seven year-long investigation. Downplaying evidence of sophistication in the preparation of the anthrax was necessary for the FBI to be able, not only to keep attention away from U.S. anthrax weaponization projects, but also to claim that the job was within Ivins' reach. But the DOJ civil division lawyers explained that the "attacker transformed liquid anthrax into an unconventional weapon." They referred to "the deadly weapon of the anthrax attacks," the "unconventional weapon," the "weapon to be sent to specified targets through the mail."

The civil division lawyers made reference to "highly specialized equipment and techniques to profoundly modify the spores in preparation for their use in the nation's first deadly attack with a pathogen." Someone, said the civil division lawyers, "had to take anthrax bacteria and cultivate it, concentrate it, dry it, and convert it into an extremely fine powder before mailing...Without each crucial step, the anthrax never could have been placed into letters, never could have been sent through the mail, and never could have been inhaled by an eventual victim such as Mr. Stevens."

> Modifications involving drying and preparation of an extremely fine powder are especially significant for purposes of foreseeability because USAMRIID exclusively used liquid anthrax spore preparations when working with viable anthrax...It would also take special expertise (even amongst those used to working with anthrax) and equipment to make dried material of the quality used in the attacks...Alteration of the form of the anthrax required technical equipment that was not routinely used for that purpose, and the equipment used to prepare the dried spore preparations that were used in the letters has never been identified.

Although the civil team's arguments were not presented explicitly in favor of Ivins' innocence, this was the direction in which they tended. It is little wonder law professor Paul Rothstein said, "I cannot think of another case in which the government has done such an egregious about-face. It destroys confidence in the criminal findings."[79] Ivins' former lawyer, Paul Kemp, said the civil case went beyond providing reasonable doubt of Ivins' guilt: it provided "millions of reasonable doubts."[80] The criticisms of the FBI's fumbling, reported extensively in mainstream media sources, showed how profoundly the Bureau's case against Bruce Ivins had deteriorated.

The filing of this motion for summary judgment by the DOJ civil division lawyers was apparently followed by panic and shouting matches within the Department. The upshot was that the civil division lawyers "got scolded" and were made to settle the case without a trial as quickly as possible.[81] The settlement discussions were initiated in August, 2011 and the final settlement was agreed to on November 28 of that year. The Stevens family received $2.5 million with no admission of liability by the U.S. government.

The *Bioterrorism & Biodefense* Articles

In 2011 and 2012 two articles co-authored by Martin Hugh-Jones, Barbara Rosenberg and Stuart Jacobsen appeared in the *Journal of Bioterrorism & Biodefense*.[82] The lead author, Hugh-Jones, is referred to in the FBI's Amerithrax Investigative Summary as a "renowned anthrax expert"—the only such expert identified by name in the Summary. The three scientists brought new evidence and new hypotheses to the discussion of the preparation of the attack spores and directly challenged the FBI's methods and conclusions.

The authors looked in their first article at the presence of tin in the attack spores. The tin had been noted before—it was part of a unique chemical signature of these spores—but the FBI had not pursued the matter and had not given an explanation of the tin's presence. The *Bioterrorism & Biodefense* authors, on the other hand, offered a hypothesis. "All the available evidence," they said, "can be explained by the hypothesis that the spore coats were silicone-coated using a tin catalyst."[83] The conclusions they drew from the "silicon-tin signature" of the attack spores were highly relevant to the search for the perpetrators of the attacks. "Potential procedures that might be applicable for silicone coating of spores, barely touched on here, are complex, highly esoteric processes that *could not possibly have been carried out by a single individual* [italics added]. They would require a laboratory with specialized capabilities and expertise not found at USAMRIID."[84] The authors clearly felt that laboratories at Battelle Memorial Institute were more likely places to look for the origin of the attack spores than was Ivins' place of work.

The challenges these researchers offered to the FBI hypothesis were reported in the mainstream press and further eroded the credibility of the FBI's case.[85]

In a second article (December, 2012) in the same journal these authors came out even more strongly in favor of a silicone microencapsulation hypothesis. They made a suggestion about the purpose of this process:

> Microencapsulation by special polymers to produce particles in the 1-10 micron range could protect microbes from environmental damage during aerosolization and delivery [e.g. via bomblets] and also from the body's initial defenses during the infection process.[86] [bracketed insertion in original]

They added that processes such as this would probably be unavailable to terrorists but could be used by a state laboratory "to produce highly effective weapons of mass destruction. "[87]

The researchers had by this time come to suspect that both tin and *B. subtilis*, a contaminant of the attack spores, originated at Dugway Proving Ground (the U.S. army testing ground in Utah),[88] and they suggested Dugway, possibly in close collaboration with Battelle, as the source of the spores. They expressed the opinion that the microencapsulated spores may not have been prepared especially for the attack letters but may have been already present in a U.S. military program, being then removed by a person, or by persons, for the 2001 attacks.[89]

In a later summation of their research they said:

> The process of spore microencapsulation requires special expertise, specific documented chemicals, and sophisticated facilities. The known clues point to Dugway or Battelle, not USAMRIID, as the site where the attack spores were prepared. Crucial evidence that would prove or disprove these points either has not been pursued or has not been released by the FBI.[90]

The cumulative effect of this research has been to further weaken the already weak case against Bruce Ivins. These weaponized spores would, presumably, have been accessible to deep insiders in U.S. intelligence and military structures, but they would certainly not have been accessible to Ivins.

Other Holes in the FBI Case

Meanwhile, other disturbing evidence continued to accumulate. For example, the FBI had claimed that Ivins could not account for extra hours in the lab in the evenings and weekends prior to the anthrax mailings. He was, they claimed, using this time to prepare the anthrax for the attacks. Such extra time in the lab at night was, they added, unprecedented in his work history.[91] But investigators for PBS Frontline, ProPublica and McClatchy Newspapers found that Ivins was doing valid and important work at the lab during the times in question. They also found that the number of night hours in the lab that had been called anomalous by the FBI were not so unusual—he had put in many extra hours in labs in the USAMRIID complex other than the lab to which the FBI had apparently, without reason, restricted its attention.[92]

The same investigators cast further doubt on the contention that Ivins had deliberately misled the FBI when making a sample submission to them. They said, basing their findings on documents made public after the NAS review, that the FBI's claim was misleading and that, moreover, the FBI knew it was misleading.[93]

Doubts about the time required to prepare the anthrax spores were also expressed by other researchers. In an interview with ProPublica, Dr. Henry Heine, a former supervisor of Ivins at USAMRIID, said that the period in Ivins' schedule identified by the FBI as his opportunity to prepare the spores (the "34 more hours in the B3 suite than his combined total for the previous seven months") was completely inadequate for the task the FBI alleges he was performing. The 34 hours, Heine said, are "more than 8,000 hours (close to a year) short of what he would have needed to grow the anthrax."[94] Heine added that it would have been impossible for Ivins to have prepared the anthrax without his colleagues being aware of it.

What, then, is the state of the DOJ's case against Ivins today? The official position of the Department and its investigative agency, the FBI, is that Ivins was the anthrax killer. The case is closed. But not only have many scientists expressed skepticism, so have several important elected officials.[95] The fact that these doubts are discussed openly in the mainstream media indicates that the standing of the DOJ's case in the courts of expert and public opinion is extremely low.[96] The much discussed "600,000 investigator work hours" and "in excess of 10,000 witness interviews" that the FBI claims to have invested in this case[97] have resulted, 13 years after the attacks, in a case without credibility.[98]

Endnotes

1 Carlos Hamann, "FBI: Anthrax Mailer More 'Unabomber' than Bin Laden," *Agence France-Presse*, November 11, 2001.

2 Ed Vulliamy, "Anthrax Attacks' 'Work of Neo-Nazis,'" *Guardian Unlimited*, October 28, 2001.

3 Guillemin, *American Anthrax: Fear, Crime, and the Investigation of the Nation's Deadliest Bioterror Attack*, 156.

4 Daschle and D'Orso, *Like No Other Time: The 107th Congress and the Two Years That Changed America Forever*, 143.

5 Ibid., 144.

6 Ibid., 177.

7 Nakashima and Weiss, "Biological Attack Concerns Spur Warnings: Restoration of Broken Public Health System Is Best Preparation, Experts Say."

8 "History Commons: 2001 Anthrax Attacks," September 22-October 2, 2001: Some People Get Sick from Anthrax, but Are Not Properly Diagnosed.

9 Schmidt and Woodward, "FBI, CIA Warn Congress of More Attacks As Blair Details Case Against Bin Laden; Retaliation Feared If U.S. Strikes Afghanistan."

10 Anderson and Loeb, "Al Qaeda May Have Crude Chemical, Germ Capabilities."

11 Rick Weiss, "Second Anthrax Case Found in Fla.; Victim's Co-Worker Infected; FBI Launches Massive Probe as Va. Monitors a Third Man," *The Washington Post*, October 9, 2001; Justin Blum and Peter Slevin, "Terrorist Ties to Anthrax Sought; No Bacteria Found in FBI Searches of Sites in Fla., Elsewhere," *The Washington Post*, October 10, 2001; Justin Blum and Peter Slevin, "Anthrax Found in Third Person; Probe Centers on Fla. Tabloid Offices Where 3 Worked," *Washington Post*, October 11, 2001; Howard Kurtz, "Anthrax Has Newsrooms On the Alert; Some Journalists Wonder If Media Are Now a Target," *The Washington Post*, October 13, 2001; Justin Blum and Michael Powell, "Anthrax Confirmed in 3rd State; Letter From Malaysia Tests Positive in Nev.; 2nd NBC Case Possible," *The Washington Post*, October 14, 2001.

12 Nakashima and Weiss, "Biological Attack Concerns Spur Warnings: Restoration of Broken Public Health System Is Best Preparation, Experts Say"; Blum and Eggen, "Crop-Dusters Thought To Interest Suspects"; Justin Blum and Rick Weiss, "Suspect May Have Wanted to Buy Plane; Inquiries Reported On Crop-Duster Loan," *The Washington Post*, September 25, 2001; Anderson and Loeb, "Al Qaeda May Have Crude Chemical, Germ Capabilities"; Rolf Myller, "Biological, Chemical Threat Is Termed Tricky, Complex; Smallpox Virus Is Most Feared in Array of Deadly Weapons," *The Washington Post*, September 30, 2001; Weiss, "Second Anthrax Case Found in Fla.; Victim's Co-Worker Infected; FBI Launches Massive Probe as Va. Monitors a Third Man"; Eggen and Woodward, "Terrorist Attacks Imminent, FBI Warns; Bush Declared Al Qaeda Is 'On the Run'; Assaults on U.S. Called Possible in 'Next Several Days.'"

13 The letter can be found on the FBI website: http://www.fbi.gov/about-us/history/famous-cases/anthrax-amerithrax/amerithrax-investigation

14 Ibid.

15 "A Nation Challenged," *The New York Times*, October 24, 2001.

16 "A Nation Challenged: Searching for a Killer," *The New York Times*, October 12, 2001, B9.

17 "Information, Please," *The New York Times*, October 16, 2001. Front page.

18 Blum and Slevin, "At Fla. Tabloid Company, a Search for Motive; First Anthrax Case, Which Ended in Photo Editor's Death, Has Investigators, Employees Asking Why"; "The Spreading Anthrax Toll," *The Washington Post*, October 24, 2001.

19 Howard Kurtz, "Powell Urges Calm in Face of New Threats; Secretary of State Refutes Taliban Contention That U.S. Raids Had Casualties," *The Washington Post*, October 22, 2001.

20 "National Security Council Directive on Office of Special Projects: NSC 10/2," June 18, 1948, http://history.state.gov/historicaldocuments/frus1945-50Intel/d292.

21 *Defense Against Weapons of Mass Destruction Act of 1996*, 1996.

22 George W. Bush, "Address to the Nation on the Terrorist Attacks," September 11, 2001, http://www.presidency.ucsb.edu/ws/?pid=58057.

23 George W. Bush, "Address to the Joint Session of the 107th Congress," in *Selected Speeches of President George W. Bush, 2001-2008*, 2001, http://georgewbush-whitehouse.archives.gov/infocus/bushrecord/documents/Selected_Speeches_George_W_Bush.pdf.

24 Charles Krauthammer, "The War: A Road Map," *The Washington Post*, September 28, 2001.

25 George F. Will, "War Without Precedent," *The Washington Post*, October 10, 2001.

26 Miller, Engelberg, and Broad, *Germs: Biological Weapons and America's Secret War*.

27 Anderson and Loeb, "Al Qaeda May Have Crude Chemical, Germ Capabilities."

28 James Woolsey, "Woolsey Interview by Wolf Blitzer" (CNN, September 11, 2001), Author's collection.

29 Juliet O'Neill, "Ex-CIA Boss Call for War on Iraq: 'Absolute Destruction' of Saddam Hussein Is next Step in War on Terrorism: Top Adviser," *Ottawa Citizen*, October 24, 2001.

30 Richard Cohen, "Public Enemy No. 2: If This Is the 'War' President Bush Says It Is, Then We Cannot Stop with Bin Laden and Al Qaeda," *The Washington Post*, October 18, 2001.

31 Robert Kagan, "Coalition of the Unwilling," *The Washington Post*, October 17, 2001.

32 David Rose and Ed Vulliamy, "Iraq 'Behind US Anthrax Outbreaks,'" *The Observer*, October 14, 2001.

33 "Review and Outlook: The Anthrax Source," *Wall Street Journal*, October 15, 2001.

34 Charles Krauthammer, "A War on Many Fronts," *The Washington Post*, October 5, 2001.

35 Blum and Slevin, "Anthrax Found in Third Person; Probe Centers on Fla. Tabloid Offices Where 3 Worked"; Rick Weiss, "Ordering Germs? There Are Hurdles First; Controls Tightened After Student Fraudulently Obtained Plague Bacterium in 1995," *The Washington Post*, October 12,

2001; Dan Eggen and Eric Pianin, "Anthrax Cases In Three Cities Share Strain," *The Washington Post*, October 20, 2001; Dan Eggen and Rick Weiss, "U.S. Says Anthrax Germ In Mail Is 'Ames' Strain; Microbe Is of Type Commonly Used in Research," *The Washington Post*, October 26, 2001.

36 "Amerithrax Investigative Summary (Released Pursuant to the Freedom of Information Act)" (United States Department of Justice, February 19, 2010).

37 Assaad references are from History Commons Anthrax Timeline, Sept 26, Oct. 2, Oct. 3.

38 Daschle and D'Orso, *Like No Other Time: The 107th Congress and the Two Years That Changed America Forever*, 172.

39 Dan Eggen and Rick Weiss, "Additive Made Spores Deadlier; 3 Nations Known to Be Able to Make Sophisticated Coating," *The Washington Post*, October 25, 2001.

40 Dan Eggen and Peter Slevin, "Germ-Laced Mail's Source Still a Mystery; Investigators Find No 'Conclusive Link' Between Anthrax Scare, Sept. 11 Attacks," *The Washington Post*, October 24, 2001.

41 "The Spreading Anthrax Toll"; Eggen and Slevin, "Germ-Laced Mail's Source Still a Mystery; Investigators Find No 'Conclusive Link' Between Anthrax Scare, Sept. 11 Attacks."

42 Eggen and Slevin, "Germ-Laced Mail's Source Still a Mystery; Investigators Find No 'Conclusive Link' Between Anthrax Scare, Sept. 11 Attacks."

43 Eggen and Weiss, "Additive Made Spores Deadlier; 3 Nations Known to Be Able to Make Sophisticated Coating."

44 Ibid.

45 "Learning on the Fly," *The Washington Post*, October 27, 2001.

46 Dan Eggen and Bob Woodward, "FBI and CIA Suspect Domestic Extremists; Officials Doubt Any Links to Bin Laden," *The Washington Post*, October 27, 2001.

47 Eggen and Weiss, "Additive Made Spores Deadlier; 3 Nations Known to Be Able to Make Sophisticated Coating."

48 Brian Ross et al., "Troubling Anthrax Additive Found," *ABCNEWS.com*, October 26, 2001.

49 Brian Ross et al., "Troubling Anthrax Additive Found; Atta Met Iraqi," *ABCNEWS.com*, October 29, 2001.

50 "Ross Responds to 'Vital Questions' About Anthrax Report," *TVNEWSER*, August 6, 2008, http://www.mediabistro.com/tvnewser/ross-responds-to-vital-questions-about-anthrax-report_b20406.

51 "History Commons: 2001 Anthrax Attacks," October 26-November 1, 2001: ABC News Heavily Pushes False Story Attempting to Link Anthrax Attacks to Iraq.

52 Glenn Greenwald, "Vital Unresolved Anthrax Questions and ABC News," *Salon*, August 1, 2008.

53 Eggen and Slevin, "Germ-Laced Mail's Source Still a Mystery; Investigators Find No 'Conclusive Link' Between Anthrax Scare, Sept. 11 Attacks."

54 Peter Slevin, "No Consensus on Who Wrote Anthrax Letters; Experts'

Speculation Covers a Broad Range," *The Washington Post*, October 25, 2001.

55 Jeff Stein, "Touch of Evil," *The Washington Post*, October 21, 2001.

56 Fred Hiatt, "Paying the Piper for Peace," *The Washington Post*, October 22, 2001.

57 Vernon Geberth and Peter Slevin, "Issues of Proof Emerge as U.S. Seeks Coalition Against Terror; Evidence Difficult to Find in Identifying State Sponsors," *The Washington Post*, September 20, 2001; Colum Lynch, "U.S. Holds Out Threat of Force Against Iraq," *The Washington Post*, October 10, 2001; Peter Finn, "Czechs Confirm Key Hijacker's 'Contact' With Iraqi Agent in Prague; Atta Communicated With Diplomat Who Was Later Expelled," *The Washington Post*, October 27, 2001; Kate Taylor, "Did Mohamed Atta Meet an Iraqi Spy in Prague?," *Slate*, September 3, 2002, http://www.slate.com/articles/news_and_politics/explainer/2002/09/did_mohamed_atta_meet_an_iraqi_spy_in_prague.html; "Mohamed Atta, the Lead 9/11 Hijacker, Did Not Meet with Iraqi Intelligence in Prague," *Leading To War*, accessed June 1, 2014, http://www.leadingtowar.com/claims_facts_atta.php.

58 Weiss, "Second Anthrax Case Found in Fla.; Victim's Co-Worker Infected; FBI Launches Massive Probe as Va. Monitors a Third Man."

59 "Mohamed Atta, the Lead 9/11 Hijacker, Did Not Meet with Iraqi Intelligence in Prague."

60 David Freed, "The Wrong Man," *The Atlantic*, May 2010, http://www.theatlantic.com/magazine/archive/2010/05/the-wrong-man/308019/.

61 Initially Ivins' death was reported as a "suspicious death" and "apparent suicide." See David Willman, "Apparent Suicide in Anthrax Case," *Los Angeles Times*, August 1, 2008. No autopsy was performed. See Edward Jay Epstein, "The Anthrax Attacks Remain Unsolved: The FBI Disproved Its Main Theory about How the Spores Were Weaponized," *Wall Street Journal*, January 24, 2010. But Guillemin, *American Anthrax*, pp. 237 ff., has an extended presentation of the evidence supporting the suicide hypothesis.

62 "Amerithrax Investigative Summary (Released Pursuant to the Freedom of Information Act)," p. 92: "Based on the evidence set forth above, the investigation into the anthrax letter attacks of 2001 has been concluded."

63 Barry Kissin, "The Truth About the Anthrax Attacks," October 2, 2009, http://www.informationclearinghouse.info/article23969.htm.

64 Glenn Greenwald, "Serious Doubt Cast on FBI's Anthrax Case against Bruce Ivins," *Salon*, February 16, 2011.

65 Committee on Review of the Scientific Approaches Used During the FBI's Investigation of the 2001 Bacillus anthracis Mailings, *Review of the Scientific Approaches Used During the FBI's Investigation of the 2001 Anthrax Letters* (Washington, D.C.: The National Academies Press, 2011).

66 Ibid, pp. 1-10; 33 ff.

67 Greg Gordon, "FBI Seeks Delay in Outside Review of Its Anthrax Probe,"

McClatchy Newspapers, December 9, 2010, http://www.mcclatchydc.com/2010/12/09/105060/fbi-seeks-delay-in-outside-review.html; Yudhijit Bhattacharjee, "New FBI Material Delays Academy Report on Anthrax Attacks," *Science*, December 10, 2010, http://news.sciencemag.org/2010/12/new-fbi-material-delays-academy-report-anthrax-attacks?ref=ra.

68 Department of Justice, Office of Public Affairs, *Justice Department and FBI Announce Formal Conclusion of Investigation into 2001 Anthrax Attacks*, Press release, (February 19, 2010), http://www.justice.gov/opa/pr/2010/February/10-nsd-166.html.

69 Greg Gordon, "Panel Supports FBI's Findings in Anthrax Letters Case," *McClatchy Washington Bureau*, March 23, 2011. A partial, redacted form of the panel's report is available: "Report of the Expert Behavioral Analysis Panel." Research Strategies Network, 2011.

70 Jeffrey Kaye, "Psychologizing Bruce Ivins: Exposing the Amerithrax Behavioral Analysis Experts," *The Public Record (TPR)*, March 26, 2011.

71 "Amerithrax Investigative Summary (Released Pursuant to the Freedom of Information Act), " pp. 75 ff.

72 Committee on Review of the Scientific Approaches Used During the FBI's Investigation of the 2001 Bacillus anthracis Mailings, *Review of the Scientific Approaches Used During the FBI's Investigation of the 2001 Anthrax Letters,* p. 147.

73 Scott Shane, "U.S. Revises Its Response to Lawsuit on Anthrax," *The New York Times*, July 19, 2011.

74 "Amerithrax Investigative Summary (Released Pursuant to the Freedom of Information Act)," p. 1.

75 Laura Sullivan, "Ivins Lawyer Rebuts DOJ Anthrax Allegations: Full NPR Interview With Ivins' Attorney Paul Kemp," NPR (National Public Radio), March 30, 2010.

76 "The scientific link between the letter material and flask number RMR-1029 is not as conclusive as stated in the DOJ Investigative Summary." "The results of the genetic analyses of the repository samples were consistent with the finding that the spores in the attack letters were derived from RMR-1029, but the analyses did not definitively demonstrate such a relationship." Committee on Review of the Scientific Approaches Used During the FBI's Investigation of the 2001 Bacillus anthracis Mailings, *Review of the Scientific Approaches Used During the FBI's Investigation of the 2001 Anthrax Letters,* p. 6.

77 For a general overview of the controversial case, see Jerry Markon, "Justice Department Takes on Itself in Probe of 2001 Anthrax Attacks," *The Washington Post*, January 27, 2012.

78 *DEFENDANT UNITED STATES' MOTION FOR SUMMARY JUDGMENT BASED ON THE ABSENCE OF PROXIMATE CAUSE AND MEMORANDUM OF LAW IN SUPPORT*, legal document, (July 15, 2011). Quotations in this section are from this document.

79 Markon, "Justice Department Takes on Itself in Probe of 2001 Anthrax Attacks."

80 Ibid.
81 Ibid.
82 Martin Hugh-Jones, Barbara Rosenberg, and Stuart Jacobsen, "The 2001 Attack Anthrax: Key Observations," *Journal of Bioterrorism & Biodefense*, October 13, 2011, http://www.omicsonline.org/2157-2526/2157-2526-S3-001.php?aid=2008; Martin Hugh-Jones, Barbara Rosenberg, and Stuart Jacobsen, "Evidence for the Source of the 2001 Attack Anthrax," *Bioterrorism & Biodefense*, December 17, 2012.
83 Hugh-Jones, Rosenberg, and Jacobsen, "The 2001 Attack Anthrax: Key Observations," 1.
84 Ibid., 9.
85 William Broad and Scott Shane, "Scientists' Analysis Disputes F.B.I. Closing of Anthrax Case," *The New York Times*, October 9, 2011.
86 Hugh-Jones, Rosenberg, and Jacobsen, "Evidence for the Source of the 2001 Attack Anthrax," 5.
87 Ibid.
88 Ibid., 1, 6.
89 Ibid., 8.
90 Barbara Rosenberg and Martin Hugh-Jones, "Scientific Data Points to Government-Made Anthrax," *Frederick News-Post*, September 15, 2013.
91 "Amerithrax Investigative Summary (Released Pursuant to the Freedom of Information Act)," pp. 29 ff.
92 This information can be found at: http://www.pbs.org/wgbh/pages/frontline/anthrax-files/
93 bid.
94 Gary Matsumoto, "Colleague Says Anthrax Numbers Add Up to Unsolved Case," *ProPublica*, April 23, 2010.
95 Carrie Johnson, "Anthrax Suspect Didn't Act Alone, Leahy Posits," *Washington Post*, September 18, 2008; Joby Warrick and Carrie Johnson, "Lawmaker 'Skeptical' Of Anthrax Results," *Washington Post*, August 1, 2009.
96 A few examples of articles in the media that have raised questions about the FBI's case: Richard Spertzel, "Bruce Ivins Wasn't the Anthrax Culprit," *The Wall Street Journal*, August 5, 2008; Eric Umansky, "Questions Linger in Ivins Anthrax Investigation," *ProPublica*, September 8, 2008; Epstein, "The Anthrax Attacks Remain Unsolved: The FBI Disproved Its Main Theory about How the Spores Were Weaponized." Matsumoto, "Colleague Says Anthrax Numbers Add Up to Unsolved Case;" Greg Gordon, "Was FBI Too Quick to Judge Anthrax Suspect the Killer?" *McClatchy Washington Bureau*, April 21, 2011; Greenwald, "Serious Doubt Cast on FBI's Anthrax Case against Bruce Ivins." Shane, "U.S. Revises Its Response to Lawsuit on Anthrax;" "Who Mailed the Anthrax Letters?" Editorial, *The New York Times*, October 17, 2011; Jerry Markon, "Justice Department Takes on Itself in Probe of 2001 Anthrax Attacks," *The Washington Post*, January 27, 2012.
97 "Amerithrax Investigative Summary (Released Pursuant to the Freedom of Information Act)," p. 4.

98 This is not meant to be a full account of the weaknesses in the case against Ivins. I have stressed recent evidence and have selected evidence I find very strong.

CHAPTER 6

ADVANCE KNOWLEDGE OF THE ATTACKS

This book argues that members of the executive branch of the U.S. government had the anthrax attacks carried out in accordance with a plan. According to this hypothesis the plan was formulated before the events of 9/11. The plan, which undoubtedly had flexibility and a set of options built into it, included the passing of legislation giving the executive increased powers and authorization to invade and occupy, at a minimum, Afghanistan and Iraq. Other associated objectives that can be assumed to have been part of the plan include increasing military spending, both in general and for biological weapons research and development. That this was a goal of the plan is borne out by the fact that the massive expansion of bioweapons R&D continues apace despite the official acknowledgement that the only bio-attack in American history, the anthrax attacks of 2001, came from inside the American program.

The present chapter explores one of the most intriguing sets of evidence in support of this hypothesis: advance knowledge of the anthrax attacks.

The October 18, 2001 issue of *The New York Times* carried a front page article by R. W. Apple Jr. entitled, "City of Power, City of Fears," in which the author says "the government has been caught completely by surprise by the anthrax attacks." This was a peculiar claim to make in *The New York Times*. Brigitte Nacos, in her book *Mass-Mediated Terrorism*, relates that her research has revealed a huge wave of advance warnings in the U.S. media, including 76 references in *The New York Times* to biological or chemical terrorism, 27 of which specifically included anthrax, between September 12 and October 3, 2001.[1] That is to say, there were a plethora of bioweapons warnings in *The New York Times* before there was supposed to have been any knowledge of an actual anthrax attack.

Of the ten most intriguing warnings in *The New York Times* in the two weeks before that newspaper reported the first anthrax case (October 5), most of the articles mention anthrax explicitly and many show the involvement of U.S. government leaders in these warnings.[2] Health Secretary Tommy Thompson, Defense Secretary Donald Rumsfeld, Attorney General John Ashcroft and White House Chief of Staff Andrew Card were among those involved. What is bound to strike an investigator looking back at the anthrax attacks is not that the government was caught off guard but that key government officials seem to have had foreknowledge of the attacks.

Yet there is a strange aura of unconcern in this matter—researchers pause briefly in puzzlement but then move on to other topics. Nacos refers in her book to "the media's sudden obsession with endlessly reporting and debating the potential for biological, chemical, and nuclear warfare in the wake of 9/11."[3] She notes that this obsession began before the reporting of the anthrax attacks and she comments:

> It was as if anchors and news experts expected the other shoe to drop as they went out of their way to report to the public that the public health system and other agencies were ill prepared to deal with bioterrorism and other mass destruction terrorism.[4]

Yet she delves no further into this odd circumstance and does not stop to examine the details of this "sudden obsession."

Jeanne Guillemin, in her substantial book on the anthrax attacks, notes:

> Anthrax was quickly identified as the most likely 'second blow' that al Qaeda would launch against Americans. My phone began ringing with requests from reporters and news stations to outline the basics about the disease. On October 4, when the diagnosis of the first anthrax letter case was announced in Florida, I was in the CBS newsroom, having come to New York, my hometown, to brief reporters.[5]

Guillemin goes on to describe the role of the media in spreading anxiety and panic with its reporting of the danger of an anthrax attack[6] and gives one of the results of this reporting: "A September 23 *Newsweek* poll indicated that eight out of ten Americans thought that a biological attack was a least 'somewhat likely.'" [7] But none of this causes Guillemin to pause to investigate this peculiar foreknowledge and its challenge to the FBI's narrative of the attacks.

The New York Times was not the only newspaper to raise concerns before there was public knowledge of the attacks. On September 15 the *Washington Post* had an article entitled, "Experts Won't Rule Out Another Attack Elsewhere in U.S." Newt Gingrich, former House speaker, warned that the second attack might use more deadly weapons: "the next stage after this will be chemical, biological and nuclear weapons." Two days later, "senior administration officials took to the airwaves to warn Americans about the possibility of a new attack in the days ahead."[8] Donald Rumsfeld noted that one should not assume the next attack would resemble the first one: "A terrorist can attack in any time and any place using a variety of different techniques."

A second article in the *Post* on the same day (September 17) had the title: "Bioterrorism: An Even More Devastating Threat." Anthrax was one of the dangers mentioned, and care was taken, in that connection, to mention Iraq. Journalist Rick Weiss added:

> Biological attacks can be far more difficult to respond to than conventional terrorist attacks. For one thing, they are covert rather than overt; for days, no one would know that one had occurred. That's a huge problem for a disease like anthrax.

Curiously, at the moment Weiss was pondering this possibility the first anthrax letters were being sent out or were about to be sent out (the first letters went out between September 17 and 18).[9]

Meanwhile, back at *The New York Times*, an op-ed by Maureen Dowd appeared on September 26 entitled, "From Botox to Botulism." The article's theme was that naïve "boomers" were living in the delusion that "they could make life safe." This generation "that came of age with psychedelic frolicking" was ill prepared, Dowd said, for Muslim martyrs dispersing biological toxins. Upper middle class New York women were carrying Cipro, Dowd claimed, in their "little black Prada techno-nylon bags" due to widespread fears of an anthrax attack.

Cipro (ciprofloxacin) was the antibiotic recommended at the time against anthrax. It is not surprising that Cipro received a great deal of media attention in October after it was clear that people were contracting anthrax, but it is odd that Cipro received so much attention in the period just prior to the attacks. On September 27, the day after Dowd's article, *The New York Times* carried an article with the title, "Anthrax Scare Prompts Run on an Antibiotic." "'We can't keep it in stock,' says Sebastian Manciameli, 'a pharmacist at Zitomer Pharmacy on Manhattan's Upper East Side.'"[10]

It eventually came out that some White House staff had been put on Cipro on September 11, 2001.[11] In 2002, the public interest group Judicial Watch filed a series of lawsuits against U.S. government agencies:

> In October, press reports revealed that White House staff had been on a regimen of the powerful antibiotic Cipro since the Sept. 11 terrorist attacks. Judicial Watch wants to know why White House workers, including President Bush, began taking the drug nearly a month before anthrax was detected on Capitol Hill.[12]

The decision to put White House staff, including George Bush and Richard Cheney, on Cipro on September 11 led to embarrassing evasions. Mr. Bush was, it seems, unwilling to tell the public he and others were on Cipro.[13]

The strange and seemingly prescient worries about anthrax were not restricted to *The New York Times* and the *Washington Post*. An investigator attempting to get a full picture of foreknowledge would want to pay attention not only to other news media, but also to other kinds of published documents[14] as well as dramatic representations. Among dramatic representations the investigator would have to deal with the planned NBC mini-series, *Terror*.[15] Work on this series was intense by August of 2001 and filming was supposed to start on September 24. The series was to have had al-Qaeda setting off an explosion in the New York subway. The event would kill 1000 people and would be accompanied by the release of anthrax. There was also a CBS series about the CIA that had been written, apparently, before September 11 and began to be broadcast in late September. One show in the series "involved a planned terrorist attack in the U.S. using anthrax." The CIA, in this story, discovers that the perpetrator intends to use "a crop duster plane to spray the deadly disease." The theme of the CBS story is said to have been suggested by a CIA consultant working with CBS.

How are we to explain all the foreknowledge of the attacks?

Presumably investigators who decline to look into this matter have an explanation that satisfies them, but they typically do not go into the issue so we are forced to speculate as to what that explanation might be. Here are four possible explanations together with responses showing their inadequacy.

Evidence and Reasonableness

Argument:

The widespread media foreknowledge of the anthrax attacks was reasonable. It was natural to think that the initial attacks of 9/11 would be followed by biological or chemical attacks—the crude WMD of terrorist groups or their state sponsors. Moreover, anthrax, the most convenient of biological agents, was possessed by some potential enemies of the U.S.

Response:

No, this foreknowledge was not reasonable. There was nothing natural or inevitable about following up airplane attacks with anthrax attacks: such a combination of events had never occurred before. Had terrorists wished to strike a second blow to the U.S. after 9/11 there were many ways they could have done it, most of them involving simple technology (guns, planes, homemade explosive devices). The conviction that anthrax attacks were natural or inevitable in the period after 9/11 was a creation of the U.S. intelligence community. To the extent that intelligence reports ascribed anthrax capacities to al-Qaeda and Iraq at this time, they were false. Neither of these parties possessed weaponized anthrax in significant quantities in 2001.

Coincidence

Argument:

There were many fears after 9/11. Biological attacks were merely one fear among many that were circulating. It is just coincidence that this particular fear turned out to be justified. There is no meaningful connection between the fears and the attacks.

Response:

It is true that biological attacks were merely one fear among many, but they received a greatly disproportionate emphasis both in the media and from government spokespeople. And this fear turned out to be uncannily justified.

Recall from Chapters 4 and 5 the numerous warnings of biological attacks, from the FBI and from assorted members of the executive branch, throughout the period when the Patriot Act was being rushed through Congress and on dates that corresponded quite precisely to major events in the passing of the bill. How was it that letters were sent to two senators directly after they resisted intense pressure from the executive? Why did so many people seem to know as soon as they heard that Stevens had anthrax that this was the result of a bioweapons attack?[16]

How do we account for comments by officials and experts that seem prescient not merely in a vague way but in a quite specific way? For example, a *Washington Post* article by Rolf Myller, dated September 30, began: "As weapons of terror, anthrax spores would be the easiest to handle."[17] Biological weapons have advantages, we are told in the article, over chemical weapons, and among biological weapons the anthrax bacterium "would be the most likely." The article concludes by saying that although terrorists working without state support might not achieve mass casualties, there is no reason to believe mass casualties are required for their ends. Alan Zelicoff of Sandia National

Laboratories in New Mexico is quoted:

> The chance of a large [bioweapons] attack that affects tens of thousands or hundreds of thousands is very small. But is that what the terrorist cares about? Inducing enough disease to produce panic or disrupt life is probably enough. I would posit that one or two cases of pulmonary anthrax in downtown Washington or New York would achieve that goal.

As the attacks unfolded the total number of casualties was, indeed, small but the panic and disruption were large. As for the timing, Robert Stevens was coming down with pulmonary anthrax precisely as Zelicoff was speaking. True, Stevens contracted the disease in Florida, but to the best of our knowledge the letters to New York were actually the first to be sent out, and the New York and Washington attacks were, as Zelicoff suggested, highly significant politically.

In some cases, presentiments and foreknowledge appear to have led to preparations that reduced the number of casualties when the attacks occurred. While casualty reduction is a good thing, this does not make the widespread *anticipation* of anthrax attacks any less perplexing.

For example, the death of Robert Stevens took place in Florida, where John Ellis Bush, ("Jeb"), the younger brother of George W. Bush, was governor. Florida's new incident commander, appointed by Jeb Bush with responsibilities for managing events in case of a terrorist attack, met with "the chief of Florida's Department of Health to confirm contingency plans in the event of a biological attack" one week before Stevens was admitted to the hospital.[18] "Also fortuitously," reported the *Washington Post*, "several laboratory chiefs from around the state had recently returned from Atlanta after attending a CDC training course in identifying bioterror agents. When the samples arrived from Bush, they had everything they needed and knew what to do."[19]

Then there is the case of Richard Cohen, a columnist for the *Washington Post*. (Cohen's cheerleading for an attack on Iraq was mentioned in Chapter 5.) Cohen wrote, in an article for *Slate* magazine in March, 2008: "I had been told soon after Sept. 11 to secure Cipro, the antidote to anthrax. The tip had come in a roundabout way from a high government official, and I immediately acted on it. I was carrying Cipro way before most people had ever heard of it."[20]

When did Cohen receive this extraordinary tip? Maureen Dowd wrote about New York women with Cipro in their Prada bags on September 25 (article published on September 26), an indication that a great many people had heard of Cipro by then. In any case, by September 26 (article published September 27) there was a run on Cipro and druggists could not keep it in stock. So Cohen's tip must have been received "way before" September 25/26 and "soon after" September 11. Whatever the precise date may have been, it was well before any government official is supposed to have known about the anthrax attacks.[21]

Note also that Cohen did not portray his anthrax information as rumor or the result of panic: it was a "tip" and it came from a high government official. What on earth can this mean? Has the FBI sought more information from Cohen? Has the Bureau asked him who his highly placed benefactor was?

Cohen has told the same story elsewhere, with the added information that when he, in the conviction that he was acting on insider information, went to his doctor to get Cipro, he found that many people had preceded him.[22]

When the FBI was pursuing Steven Hatfill and building a case against him it did not hesitate to cite his use of Cipro prior to the anthrax attacks as evidence of his complicity in the crime.[23] Have Cohen and his source been treated in the same way?

Error

Argument:

Government officials and experts estimated that anthrax attacks were possible or even likely, based on the intelligence they had received from various agencies. They made their best call and began warning of the dangers of such attacks. The intelligence they provided was sound insofar as anthrax attacks actually occurred; it was weak insofar as it misidentified the source of the attacks.

Response:

If error is chosen as an option, it will have to be complete error, not partial error. If a physician gives a prognosis, saying that a man will die in a week from cancer, and the man dies in a week when a building collapses on him, the doctor does not get to claim half-credit. He or she can claim no credit whatsoever. For the same reasons, the intelligence community gets no points for predicting the anthrax attacks since the attacks, when they came, issued from a completely different source, and therefore presumably via different routes, methods and motives, than the intelligence community, obsessed with al-Qaeda and Iraq, had predicted.

The error explanation cannot, in any case, stand up to scrutiny. As in the previous case, the explanation looks sensible only when given in vague terms. The fact is that parties known to have deceived the U.S. population repeatedly and intentionally during the period in question gave out, as "intelligence," warnings that had no sound empirical foundation and that served the interests of these parties. This becomes apparent as soon as we restore the attacks of the fall of 2001 to their proper context.

The Double Perpetrator hypothesis not only aimed at pointing to a ubiquitous and shadowy enemy ("al-Qaeda"), but also sought to frame Iraq. Iraq was, according to this hypothesis, both supporting al-Qaeda and in possession of weapons of mass destruction. But we know that these two claims about Iraq were part of a program of systematic, intentional deception that stretched over several years.

Here are three well-known sets of evidence that combine to make this clear.

(i) The Center for Public Integrity and the associated Fund for Independence in Journalism carried out a lengthy and detailed study of public statements made by leading members of the Bush administration. The results of the study were released in 2008.[24] The study examined statements made by eight top Bush administration officials: President G. W. Bush, Vice President Dick Cheney, Secretary of State Colin Powell, National Security Advisor Condoleezza Rice, Defense Secretary Donald Rumsfeld, Deputy Defense Secretary Paul Wolfowitz, White House Press Secretary Ari Fleischer, and White House Press Secretary Scott McClellan. The two-year period studied stretched from September 11, 2001 to September 11, 2003. Two topics were the basis of study: (a) "Iraq's possession of weapons of mass destruction" and (b) "Iraq's links to Al Qaeda."

The study, which produced a searchable database, discovered that on at least 532 occasions these officials made at least 935 false statements on these two topics.

The database not only counts the false statements but "juxtaposes what President Bush and these seven top officials were saying for public consumption against what was known, or should have been known, on a day-to-day basis."

The researchers concluded that "the statements were part of an orchestrated campaign that effectively galvanized public opinion and, in the process, led the nation to war under decidedly false pretenses."

The incidence of false statements peaked twice, first in August 2002, at the time of "congressional consideration of a war resolution," and, second, when Colin Powell went to the UN Security Council to make the case for war against Iraq. The day of the second and higher peak is captured in the well known image of Colin Powell holding in the air a vial of simulated anthrax for the UN Security Council to ponder.

These peaks remind us of the storm of warnings about terrorist attacks involving biological or chemical weapons that clustered around the consideration of the Patriot Act by Congress. Apparently there are certain moments that call for an intensification of deception.

In addition to the 935 false statements, "Bush and these seven top officials also made hundreds of other statements in the two years after 9/11 in which they implied that Iraq had weapons of mass destruction or links to Al Qaeda." In other words, in addition to directly false statements, innuendo and misleading statements were common.

(ii) The original "Downing Street Memo" consists of minutes of a meeting held on July 23, 2002 at which U.K. Prime Minister Tony Blair met with senior ministers involved in establishing that country's Iraq policy.[25]

The document is indicative, quite precisely, of a conspiracy. The document reveals *multiple persons* meeting to consider and develop a *plan* to facilitate the commission of an *illegal* action by devising its propaganda legitimization—the *casus belli* for the illegal invasion of Iraq. The illegality of the action that the plan intends to support is acknowledged more than once in the minutes and the Foreign Secretary is delegated the job of working up a plan to allow the invasion to go ahead with a show of legality. *Secrecy* is also key to the meeting and the plan, as indicated by the word "SECRET" on the document as well as the words: "This record is extremely sensitive. No further copies should be made."

The document also makes reference to the earlier and larger conspiracy, namely the conspiracy of the Bush administration to proceed to a war against Iraq. It is clearly said in the Downing Street Memo that the Bush administration had already decided (by July 23, 2002) to go to war against Iraq and that it had also decided to do so through deception. "Bush wanted to remove Saddam, through military action, justified by the conjunction of terrorism and WMD. But the intelligence and facts were being fixed around the policy. The NSC had no patience with the UN route..." These two claims by the head of MI6, the U.K. foreign intelligence service, mean (a) that the same two claims central to the Double Perpetrator scheme familiar from the anthrax attacks would soon be central to the invasion of Iraq, namely support for terrorism and possession of WMD, and (b) that the claims were not justified by evidence and were being used as a pretext for war.

Later in the same document the legal case for war is said to be "thin." The Attorney General makes it clear that there is, in fact, no justification in international law for an invasion of Iraq. Nonetheless, one conclusion of the meeting is: "We should work on the assumption that the UK would take part in any military action." The anticipated legal problem was to be addressed by working up an ultimatum (on the otherwise largely irrelevant inspections issue) to Saddam Hussein: if he rejected it—the hoped-for outcome—there might be a basis for a legal justification of the invasion.

Law was viewed as something to circumvent in order to avoid negative consequences.

(iii) In April of 2009 a redacted version of a 2008 report by the Senate Armed Services Committee was made public. One of the revelations was that an objective of the torture carried out on detainees in the Global War on Terror was to obtain testimony that would support the administration's claimed link between al-Qaeda and Iraq. U.S. Army psychiatrist Major Paul Burney said, "a large part of the time we were focused on trying to establish a link between Al Qaeda and Iraq and were not being successful in establishing a link between Al Qaeda and Iraq...there was more and more pressure to resort to measures that might produce more immediate results."[26]

A number of senior officials in the Bush administration were implicated. Jonathan Landay of McClatchy Newspapers reported that "Cheney's and Rumsfeld's people were told repeatedly, by CIA...and by others, that there wasn't any reliable intelligence that pointed to operational ties between bin Laden and Saddam, and that no such ties were likely because the two were fundamentally enemies, not allies."[27]

As with the military tribunals, a set of questions can be asked: why use techniques (torture in this case) that are known to be unreliable in discovering truth?[28] Why risk losing the battle for "hearts and minds" by confirming the worst views of the behavior of the United States? Why risk losing the support of key allies by violating international law and common standards of decency? Why had Cheney and Rumsfeld been willing to push so hard to establish this link? As with the military tribunals, the answer emerges when one understands the fraudulent nature of the two sets of attacks that took place in the fall of 2001. Although the McClatchy article suggests that abusive tactics were used to "seek" an "Iraq-al Qaida link,"[29] the administration was not concerned to "seek" a link. It was trying to obtain statements, by force, that would "prove" false claims. The resort to torture did not seek truth any more than the military tribunals sought truth.

In short, the contention that al-Qaeda and Iraq were linked as terrorist-to-sponsor—the Double Perpetrator hypothesis— was false, was known to be false, and flowed from repeated acts of deception by the U.S. government during this period, rather than from error.

Information control

Argument:

Suppose state officials, not wanting to cause panic in

citizens, initially concealed part of what they knew. Suppose, for example, the FBI actually discovered that there was a case of cutaneous anthrax in mid-September? Or perhaps the Bureau even discovered a letter at this time with anthrax spores? In either case, perhaps a decision was made to conceal these facts in order to break the news more gently to the public via indirect and circuitous warnings? In this case, even if the officials' actions were ill-advised there is no question of the officials themselves being involved in the attacks.

Response:

It is not surprising that the U.S. administration did not take this escape route. Legal action in 2002 by Judicial Watch had already raised the issue of the White House receiving Cipro on September 11 while leaving other citizens to fend for themselves. How could the administration avoid the charge that it was responsible for five deaths and many injuries from anthrax by having chosen to keep the population uninformed?

But there is a more convincing reason to reject this explanation. At best this explanation could deal with foreknowledge over a period of perhaps two weeks prior to the news of Stevens' disease. It certainly cannot deal with foreknowledge that precedes September 11, 2001.

In the following two chapters several cases suggestive of such foreknowledge will be discussed. The present chapter will close with one such case.

Dark Winter

During June 22-23, 2001, less than three months before the initiation of the anthrax attacks, several institutions joined to sponsor a biological warfare simulation at Andrews Air Force Base. The exercise, called Dark Winter, involved a scenario where terrorists release smallpox virus, via aerosol spray, in three American cities, beginning in early December, 2002. By the time of the Christmas holidays of 2002, 16,000 smallpox cases are reported in 25 states. The disease has by this time also spread to 10 other countries.[30]

Biological weapons attacks are frequently simulated as part of preparedness training, so there is nothing inherently suspect about such an exercise. Moreover, such simulations can be expected to share certain common elements. But the cumulative parallels between this particular simulation and the actual anthrax attacks are worthy of note. Consider the following ten elements common to both Dark Winter and the anthrax attacks:[31]

(i) *Dark Winter:* Anonymous letters are sent to the mainstream media. The letters contain threats, including threats of follow-up attacks with anthrax. In addition, the strain of smallpox in the epidemic is identifiable since "each letter also contained a genetic fingerprint of the smallpox strain matching the fingerprint of the strain causing the current epidemic."

Anthrax Attacks: Anonymous letters are sent to the mainstream media. Some contain threats and harmless powder while others contain threats and anthrax spores. From the spores it is possible to determine the genetic strain of the anthrax.

(ii) *Dark Winter:* Among the casualties is a high state official. The U.S. President gives the following announcement: "Good morning. I am sorry to announce that the Secretary of State is ill. He has been hospitalized at Bethesda Naval Hospital. I know all of our prayers are with him."

Anthrax Attacks: Letters with anthrax spores are sent to two prominent U.S. senators.

(iii) *Dark Winter:* Osama Bin Laden is on the list of suspects. Reference is made to the possibility of "autonomous groups—specifically Bin Laden." (An October 23 *Washington Post* article, describing the Dark Winter terrorist teams, says: "spookily prescient, they are identified as being from al Qaeda."[32])

Anthrax Attacks: Bin Laden's group is an immediate and leading suspect and remains so for some time.

(iv) *Dark Winter:* As the attacks proceed, the nature of the perpetrators starts to emerge: "There is a very high probability this attack was conducted by either a state or a state-sponsored international terrorist organization."

Anthrax Attacks: The Double Perpetrator scenario is gradually unveiled.

(v) *Dark Winter:* In a memo to the Director of Central Intelligence and the Director of the FBI, the list of key suspect states is said to be short: there are five suspects, and Iraq is one.

Anthrax Attacks: As the anthrax spores are studied a state supplier is said to be indicated, and the list of possible suppliers is said to be very short. Iraq is on the list.

(vi) *Dark Winter:* A "prominent Iraqi defector is claiming that Iraq arranged the bioweapons attacks on the US through intermediaries."

Anthrax Attacks: Many WMD claims are made by Iraqi defectors. On October 11, as the perpetrators of the anthrax attacks are being sought, the *Washington Post* carries an article on one such defector, remarking: "[Khidhir] Hamza knows too well that if the terrorist network that hit the World Trade Center and the Pentagon has access to nuclear and biological weapons, it is probably through Iraq, through the weapons program that he headed until his escape in 1994."[33]

(vii) *Dark Winter:* Preparations are made for drastic restrictions of civil liberties in the U.S., possibly to include

Martial Rule, which may be imposed if "a crisis threatens to undermine the stability of the U.S. Government." "Options for martial rule include, but are not limited to, prohibition of free assembly, national travel ban, quarantine of certain areas, suspension of the writ of habeas corpus [i.e., arrest without due process], and/or military trials in the event that the court system becomes dysfunctional." (Material in square brackets is in the original.)

Anthrax Attacks: The Patriot Act is rushed through Congress with the help of the attacks and related threats, while the NSA begins mass domestic spying. Military tribunals are then established for trying suspects.

(viii) *Dark Winter:* Citizens panic and begin imploring the state for a medical solution: "Mothers Plead for Vaccine as Supply Dwindles."

Anthrax Attacks: On the day after the first anthrax death, a *Washington Post* article claims that the desire for antibiotics is so strong that, "[p]eople are on their hands and knees begging for drugs."[34] The article's author, Rick Weiss, wrote as early as September 28, before the news of the anthrax attacks broke, about the need for a publicly available anthrax vaccine.[35]

(ix) *Dark Winter:* Assaults and harassment are directed by parts of the population against citizens of presumed Arab ethnicity. "Reports of beatings and harassment of persons of dark skin and of Arab Americans are increasing in numbers and violence."

Anthrax Attacks: In the fall of 2001, there is a wave of aggressive acts in the United States, ranging from name-calling to murder, directed against residents of suspected Arab ethnicity.[36] The wave of violence is, apparently, connected mainly to the 9/11 attacks, but prejudices are reinforced when the anthrax attacks are blamed on al-Qaeda and Iraq.

(x) *Dark Winter:* Near the end of the simulation there is confirmation that the United States has been attacked by a particular double perpetrator. The news anchor for (fictional) TV corporation NCN announces: "Still no group claims responsibility for unleashing the deadly smallpox virus, but NCN has learned that Iraq may have provided the technology behind the attack to terrorist groups based in Afghanistan."[37]

Anthrax Attacks: As explained in Chapter 5, this conclusion is the one that a powerful party within the U.S. pushes for, especially in the second half of October, 2001.

Dark Winter Players

In addition to the above parallels between the Dark Winter simulation and the anthrax attacks that soon followed, there was a strange intersection of roles. Consider Judith Miller, James Woolsey and Jerome Hauer. In Dark Winter, Miller played a reporter for *The New York Times*, Woolsey played the director of the CIA, and Hauer played director of the Federal Emergency Management Agency (FEMA).

Judith Miller would have found it easy to play a reporter for *The New York Times* since that was her real-life role as well. Mention was made in Chapter 5 of an article in *The New York Times* on October 26 that she co-wrote with William Broad that touched on the bentonite claims ABC was more flagrantly publicizing at the same time, used in both cases to implicate Iraq. But this was a minor part of her participation in the framing of Iraq. Her bioweapons book, *Germs* (co-authored with William Broad and Stephen Engelberg),[38] which sounded warnings about Iraq's alleged ongoing bioweapons program, was published just as the anthrax attacks were about to enter public consciousness (probably on October 2, the day the first inhalation anthrax victim entered the hospital).[39] By the end of October the book was a *New York Times* best seller, an effective and timely piece of propaganda against Iraq.[40] On October 12—the same day anthrax was reported at NBC—Miller was the recipient of a bioweapon-threat letter at her office at *The New York Times*. The powder she received was harmless but she was able to write with flair about the incident.[41] No doubt the scare promoted sales of her book.

Miller was an important player in the promotion of war with Iraq. Her use of false information about Iraq's weapons of mass destruction was extremely useful to the Bush administration in the lead-up to the 2003 invasion. Journalist Alex Pareene has put the matter bluntly:

> She was hyping bullshit stories about Iraq's WMD capabilities as far back as 1998, and in the run-up to the war, her front-page scoops were cited by the Bush administration as evidence that Saddam needed to be taken out, right away...[42]

The New York Times, embarrassed when her fraudulent stories were discredited, finally cut her loose in 2005.

James Woolsey would also have found it easy to play his role in Dark Winter. He had been the actual director of the CIA under the Clinton administration. The Institute for Policy Studies noted:

> Woolsey was an outspoken proponent of invading Iraq even before 9/11. As a supporter of the Project for the New American Century (PNAC), the influential letterhead group founded by William Kristol and Robert Kagan to champion a 'Reaganite policy of military strength and moral clarity,' Woolsey signed several PNAC open letters to government figures encouraging an aggressive military agenda. One such letter was PNAC's 1998 missive to Clinton, which served as the

opening salvo in neoconservative efforts to support a U.S. invasion of Iraq.[43]

Woolsey began trying to implicate Iraq in the 9/11 attacks on the day itself and continued doing so thereafter.[44] When the anthrax attacks unfolded, he added them to the list of Iraq's likely crimes, telling the American Jewish Congress on October 22, 2001 that a war against Iraq should be waged quickly and "ruthlessly."[45]

But Woolsey was not content to frame Iraq. He also played an important role in the wave of Islamophobia that hit the United States after the fall attacks. He gave his support to such scurrilous productions as the volume *Shariah: The Threat to America*[46] and the DVD "The Third Jihad: Radical Islam's Vision for America."[47]

Woolsey's work in the post-9/11 period also led to public accusations that he had profited financially from the boom in military spending.[48]

Jerome Hauer, who played FEMA director in Dark Winter, was, in real life, an important figure in the linking of the 9/11 attacks and the anthrax attacks. Hauer is a member of The Committee on the Present Danger, described by the Institute for Policy Studies as "a neoconservative pressure group."[49] A committee of this same name played an important anti-Soviet role during the Cold War, while the present incarnation of the committee was launched in 2004 to promote the Global War on Terror.

Hauer has a Master's degree in emergency medical services from Johns Hopkins and maintains a deep interest in bioterrorism. On 9/11 he "was a national security advisor with the Department of Health and Human Services, a managing director with Kroll Associates, and a guest on national television, because of his background in counter-terror and his specialized knowledge of biological warfare."[50]

Hauer participated in the U.S. administration's efforts, on September 30 and October 1, 2001, to sound warning bells about biological weapons attacks as part of the effort to intimidate Congress into the passing of the Patriot Act by October 5.[51]

But Hauer was more than an expert in bioterrorism. He had been the director of the Office of Emergency Management (OEM) of New York City from 1996 until early in 2000.[52] The OEM had been located in a "bunker" on the 23rd floor of World Trade Center 7. It was while he was working at this job that many New Yorkers first learned of him.

An article in *The New York Times* on July 27, 1999 explained that when he was 15, Hauer's mother, a hospital vice president, "helped him get a job in the hospital's morgue," where he was responsible for "cutting open the gut and cleaning it and pinning it and making it ready for the pathologist to review."[53] Making the most of the metaphor, the *Times* author said that Hauer, "likes guts...viscera, innards, the stuff things are made of." By 1999, the article continued, Hauer had graduated from actual human guts to the innards of structures. His obsession had become building collapse. Hauer, said the article, collected samples from every building collapse he could find in New York.

Presumably Hauer was in his element when, two years later, he got a chance to become intimately familiar with what were arguably the most politically important building collapses in modern history. Not only did the Twin Towers undergo a surprising annihilation, but Hauer's old bailiwick, World Trade Center 7, although not hit by a plane, disappeared that day as well. The OEM bunker was supposed to be the command center for response to terrorism, but on 9/11 it was abandoned early in the morning. Then the entire 47-story building underwent a sudden collapse--allegedly from fire, although no steel-framed skyscraper had ever come down in such a fashion before except from controlled demolition—at near free-fall acceleration at 5:21 p.m.[54]

Interviewed by Dan Rather on television on September 11, 2001, Hauer's anticipation of what the official causes would be for the destruction of the twin towers—weakening of the structures through plane impact and burning jet fuel—has surprised many. [55] He likewise reported on television on the same day (ABC News, in an interview with Peter Jennings), well before World Trade 7's collapse, that he had heard concerns about the "structural stability of the building." This is merely one instance among many of suspect foreknowledge of this historically unprecedented collapse.[56]

The Dark Winter Designer

A key designer of Dark Winter was Tara O'Toole, who was later chosen by the Obama administration as undersecretary of science and technology for the Department of Homeland Security. O'Toole has been severely criticized for her bioterrorism exercises. One scientist (chemist George Smith) has referred to her as "the top academic/salesperson for the coming of apocalyptic bioterrorism which has never quite arrived. [She's] most prominent for always lobbying for more money for biodefense, conducting tabletop exercises on bioterrorism for easily overawed public officials, exercises tweaked to be horrifying."[57] Another scientist, Rutgers University microbiologist Richard Ebright, has commented that "O'Toole supported every flawed decision and counterproductive policy on biodefense, biosafety, and biosecurity during the Bush administration."[58]

Foreknowledge Summary

Attempts to solve a crime depend on pattern recognition. Patterns do not always indicate causal connections and there is no way to be certain Dark Winter and the anthrax attacks were connected in a substantial way—that they were, for example, both part of a general plan created by one group or linked groups. Still, given the failure of official investigating agencies in the U.S. to carry out their investigations fully and responsibly, civil society researchers have no choice but to attempt the job. The parallels between Dark Winter and the anthrax attacks are sufficiently suspect to warrant further investigation.

It is difficult, in fact, when reviewing Dark Winter and its participants, to avoid a feeling of vertigo. Perhaps the contrast between simulation and reality is misleading? Perhaps the anthrax attacks were the second phase of a simulation—a phase in which lethality would give the simulation and its purposes the attention the designers craved?

In any case, foreknowledge of the anthrax attacks, widely accepted in the fall of 2001 as deriving from a valid process of intelligence gathering, is today a highly visible sign of fraud. The foreknowledge did not derive from valid intelligence gathering, and because we now know this, we are justified in assuming it derived from the perpetrators of the attacks. An intelligence agency with integrity would be able to follow the leads, even today, quickly to their sources.

Endnotes

1 Brigitte Nacos, *Mass-Mediated Terrorism: The Central Role of the Media in Terrorism and Counterterrorism*, 2nd ed. (Lanham: Rowman & Littlefield, 2007), 65.

2 The following are the ten most important articles.

i. "Nation's Civil Defense Could Prove to Be Inadequate Against a Germ or Toxic Attack." Sept. 23, 2001.
ii. "Crop-Dusters Are Grounded on Fears of Toxic Attacks." Sept. 25, 2001.
iii. "The Specter of Biological Terror." Sept. 26, 2001.
iv. "From Botox to Botulism." Sept. 26, 2001.
v. "Anthrax Scare Prompts Run on an Antibiotic." Sept. 27, 2001.
vi. "Big Push to Accelerate Vaccine Effort." Sept. 28, 2001.
vii. "Some Experts Say U.S. Is Vulnerable To A Germ Attack." Sept. 30, 2001.
viii. "Defense Secretary Warns Of Unconventional Attacks". Oct. 1, 2001, B5.
ix. "Health Secretary Testifies About Germ Warfare Defenses." Oct. 4, 2001.
x. "E.P.A. Years Behind Timetable On Guarding Water From At-

tack." Oct. 4, 2001.

3 Nacos, *Mass-Mediated Terrorism: The Central Role of the Media in Terrorism and Counterterrorism*, 65.

4 Ibid.

5 Guillemin, *American Anthrax: Fear, Crime, and the Investigation of the Nation's Deadliest Bioterror Attack*, xx–xxi.

6 Ibid., 50.

7 Ibid.

8 John F. Harris, "Bush Gets More International Support For U.S. 'Crusade' Against Terrorism; Officials Warn New Attacks Are Possible," *The Washington Post*, September 17, 2001.

9 "History Commons: 2001 Anthrax Attacks," September 17-18, 2001: First Wave of Anthrax Attacks Targets ABC, NBC, CBS, New York Post, and National Enquirer.

10 Lewin, "Anthrax Scare Prompts Run on an Antibiotic."

11 Sandra Sobierai, "White House Mail Machine Has Anthrax," *Washington Post*, October 23, 2001.

12 "Feds Sued Over Anthrax Documents: Legal Group Wonders Why White House Took Cipro before Attacks," *WorldNetDaily*, June 7, 2002. http://www.wnd.com/2002/06/14170/.

13 Mike Allen, "Bush Balks at Antrax-Test Question; But President States 3 Times That He Does Not Have the Disease," *The Washington Post*, October 24, 2001; "The Anthrax Crisis," *The Washington Post*, October 26, 2001.

14 See, for example, Philipp Sarasin, *Anthrax: Bioterror as Fact and Fantasy* (Cambridge, Massachusetts: Harvard Univ. Press, 2006), p. 118.

15 For the discussion of these two mini-series I am indebted to the blogger who goes under the name of "Shoestring." See "The CBS Drama Series That--With CIA Help--Predicted 9/11 and the Anthrax Attacks," *Shoestring 9/11: Investigating 9/11 and Other Acts of the Secret State*, June 19, 2013, http://www.shoestring911.blogspot.ca/.

16 Krauthammer, "A War on Many Fronts"; Jo Becker and Rick Weiss, "Problems in Bioterror Response; First Cases Show Need to Inform Public and Guard Against Panic," *The Washington Post*, October 14, 2001.

17 Myller, "Biological, Chemical Threat Is Termed Tricky, Complex; Smallpox Virus Is Most Feared in Array of Deadly Weapons."

18 Becker and Weiss, "Problems in Bioterror Response; First Cases Show Need to Inform Public and Guard Against Panic."

19 Ibid.

20 Richard Cohen, "How Did I Get Iraq Wrong?" *Slate*, March 18, 2008.

21 Robert Stevens' pulmonary anthrax was diagnosed on October 3. This was the first time actual anthrax (either the substance or the disease) could have been made known either to the FBI or to anyone else in authority. The first letters with anthrax were postmarked on September 18 but no one except the perpetrators is supposed to have known about the anthrax in these letters for some time. NBC personnel have claimed

that, after two suspect letters were received (a September 18 Trenton, New Jersey letter and a September 20 St. Petersburg, Florida threat letter), they alerted the FBI on September 25. The Bureau supposedly picked up the St. Petersburg letter on September 26 but did not test the enclosed powder--which contained no anthrax--until some days later. The Bureau has said it did not receive the Trenton letter, containing actual anthrax, until October 12, which is also the day an announcement was made that NBC employee Erin O'Connor had tested positive for cutaneous anthrax after handling the two letters. Eric Lipton and Jim Rutenberg, "Wider Anthrax Reports, but No Link Is Found," *The New York Times*, October 14, 2001.

22 Richard Cohen, "Our Forgotten Panic," *The Washington Post*, July 22, 2004. For crucial timeline information the History Commons chronology of events is extremely helpful. For example, Cohen is dealt with at:http://www.historycommons.org/timeline.jsp?anthraxattacks_other=anthraxattacks_cipro___bayer&timeline=anthraxattacks

23 "Amerithrax Investigative Summary (Released Pursuant to the Freedom of Information Act)," p. 20.

24 Charles Lewis and Mark Reading-Smith, "False Pretenses: Following 9/11, President Bush and Seven Top Officials of His Administration Waged a Carefully Orchestrated Campaign of Misinformation about Saddam Hussein's Iraq," January 23, 2008, http://www.publicintegrity.org/2008/01/23/5641/false-pretenses.

25 "The Downing Street Memo(s)," accessed May 14, 2014, http://downingstreetmemo.com/.

26 *Inquiry Into The Treatment Of Detainees In U.S. Custody: Report Of The Committee On Armed Services, United States Senate*, November 20, 2008, 41, http://media.mcclatchydc.com/smedia/2009/04/21/20/Detainees-main1.source.prod_affiliate.91.pdf.

27 Jonathan Landay, "Report: Abusive Tactics Used to Seek Iraq-Al Qaeda Link," *McClatchy Newspapers*, April 21, 2009.

28 *Inquiry Into The Treatment Of Detainees In U.S. Custody: Report Of The Committee On Armed Services, United States Senate*, 6.

29 Landay, "Report: Abusive Tactics Used to Seek Iraq-Al Qaeda Link."

30 "DARK WINTER: Bioterrorism Exercise, Andrews Air Force Base, June 22-23, 2001 (Final Script--Dark Winter Exercise)" (Johns Hopkins Center for Civilian Biodefense, Center for Strategic and International Studies, ANSER, Memorial Institute for the Prevention of Terrorism, 2001), http://www.upmchealthsecurity.org/our-work/events/2001_dark-winter/Dark%20Winter%20Script.pdf; Steve Fainaru and Joby Warrick, "Bioterrorism Preparations Lacking at Lowest Levels; Despite Warnings and Funds, Local Defenses Come Up Short," *The Washington Post*, October 22, 2001.

31 "DARK WINTER: Bioterrorism Exercise, Andrews Air Force Base, June 22-23, 2001 (Final Script--Dark Winter Exercise)."

32 Roxanne Roberts, "A War Game to Send Chills Down the Spine," *The Washington Post*, October 23, 2001.

33 Marc Fisher, "To Stop Terror Defang Saddam, Defector Says," *The Washington Post*, October 11, 2001.

34 Weiss, "Source of Florida Anthrax Case Is Sought; Victim Dies as 50 Investigators Search."

35 Weiss, "Demand Growing for Anthrax Vaccine: Fear of Bioterrorism Attack Spurs Requests for Controversial Shot."

36 *Department of Justice Oversight: Preserving Our Freedoms While Defending Against Terrorism*, 402 ff.; Sheehi, *Islamophobia: The Ideological Case Against Muslims*.

37 *Dark Winter Simulated Newscasts*, n.d., http://www.upmchealthsecurity.org/our-work/events/2001_dark-winter/dark_winter_slideshow.html.

38 Miller, Engelberg, and Broad, *Germs: Biological Weapons and America's Secret War*.

39 Support can be found for several differing dates of publication of this book, but the confusion is not important for my purposes since I am not claiming the book's publication was timed to fit the attacks to the day, simply that its appearance near the beginning of the anthrax attacks is suspicious. In any case, the October 2 publication date seems the most common, as noted here: http://en.wikipedia.org/wiki/Germs:_Biological_Weapons_and_America%27s_Secret_War. The October 2 date seems also implied in the following review: Simon Wessely, "Weapons of Mass Hysteria," *The Guardian*, October 20, 2001. http://www.guardian.co.uk/education/2001/oct/20/highereducation.news1/print. *The Guardian*'s reviewer notes that, "With faultless timing, it was published just four days before news of the Florida anthrax cases broke." I am assuming Wessely is taking Oct. 6, the day Stevens' death from anthrax was reported in the media, as the day the news of the Florida cases broke.

40 Alexander Cockburn, "Judy Miller's War," *CounterPunch*, August 16, 2003.

41 Miller's participation in Dark Winter is noted in the Dark Winter "Exercise Summary." As of May 28, 2013 this was available here: http://www.upmchealthsecurity.org/website/events/2001_darkwinter/summary.html. Miller received the anthrax threat letter from St. Petersburg on October 12, 2001, and this was reported in *The New York Times* on Oct. 13. She wrote about it the next day: Judith Miller, "Fear Hits Newsroom in a Cloud of Powder," *The New York Times*, October 14, 2001.

42 Alex Pareene, "Judith Miller: From the Times to the Nuts"," *Salon*, December 30, 2010.

43 "Right Web: Tracking Militarists' Efforts to Influence U.S. Foreign Policy: James Woolsey (last Updated Nov. 12, 2013)," *Institute for Policy Studies*, n.d., http://www.rightweb.irc-online.org/profile/woolsey_james.

44 Ibid. Woolsey named Iraq as a suspect on CNN in the evening of 9/11.

45 O'Neill, "Ex-CIA Boss Call for War on Iraq: 'Absolute Destruction' of Saddam Hussein Is next Step in War on Terrorism: Top Adviser."

46 *Sharia: The Threat to America (An Exercise in Competitive Analysis-*

-Report of Team B II) (Washington, D.C.: The Center for Security Policy, 2010).

47 Wayne Kopping, *The Third Jihad: Radical Islam's Vision for America*, DVD (Clarion Fund, 2008).

48 "Right Web: Tracking Militarists' Efforts to Influence U.S. Foreign Policy: James Woolsey (last Updated Nov. 12, 2013)"; Steve Clemons, "Woolsey Watch: Woolsey Needs to Make a Choice Between Being a War Profiteer or War Pundit," *Washington Note*, n.d., http://washingtonnote.com/woolsey_watch_w_1/; Bruce Bigelow, "Enlisting Locals: Small Defense Firms such as ISL Thrive with Military Contracts," *San Diego Union-Tribune*, July 8, 2005.

49 "Right Web: Tracking Militarists' Efforts to Influence U.S. Foreign Policy: Committee on the Present Danger," *Institute for Policy Studies*, n.d., http://www.rightweb.irc-online.org/profile/committee_on_the_present_danger.

50 "Jerome Hauer," *Wikipedia*, accessed May 26, 2014, https://en.wikipedia.org/wiki/Jerome_Hauer.

51 *Much To Be Done to Protect US From Bio-Terror Attack* (New York-WABC, October 1, 2001).

52 "Jerome Hauer," *Wikipedia*.

53 Randy Kennedy, "What Could Go Wrong? It's His Job to Know," *The New York Times*, July 27, 1999.

54 David Griffin, *The Mysterious Collapse of World Trade Center 7: Why the Final Official Report about 9/11 Is Unscientific and False* (Northampton, Mass.: Olive Branch Press, 2010).

55 Kevin Ryan, "Demolition Access To The WTC Towers: Part Two-Security," *911 Truth.org*, August 13, 2009, http://www.911truth.org/demolition-access-to-the-wtc-towers-part-two-security/.

56 "9/11/01: OEM Director Jerome Hauer Explains Abandoning WTC 7..." (ABC News), accessed May 26, 2014, https://www.youtube.com/watch?v=MKFPaqq7cA4; Griffin, *The Mysterious Collapse of World Trade Center 7: Why the Final Official Report about 9/11 Is Unscientific and False*.

57 Noah Shachtman, "DHS' New Chief Geek Is a Bioterror 'Disaster,' Critics Charge," *WIRED*, May 6, 2009, http://www.wired.com/2009/05/dhs-new-geek-in-chief-is-a-biodefense-disaster-critics-say/.

58 Ibid.

CHAPTER 7

THE HIJACKER CONNECTION

The claim that the anthrax attacks were the result of a high level domestic conspiracy in the U.S. will be shocking to some readers, but it will probably be less shocking than the companion claim that the domestic group that perpetrated this crime was *linked to, or identical with*, the perpetrators of the 9/11 attacks. But if we are committed to following the anthrax evidence wherever it may lead, we will find ourselves among the 19 Hijackers of 9/11 fame.

The Florida Connection

At least 15 of the 19 Hijackers had a connection to Florida.[1] The main area of their activity was along the southeast coast between West Palm Beach and Miami. The first person to die from anthrax, Robert Stevens, perished in Boca Raton, in the midst of this short strip, roughly 71 miles long.[2] Was there a connection between the first anthrax death and the Hijackers? The answer is Yes.

Anthrax victim Robert Stevens worked as a photo editor for a tabloid in Boca Raton called the *Sun*.[3] (The *Sun*, now defunct, was owned by American Media Inc., which also owns the *National Enquirer*.) The editor-in-chief of the *Sun* was a man named Mike Irish, whose wife Gloria had a direct connection to two of the Hijackers. Gloria Irish was a real estate agent and she had found apartments, in the summer of 2001, for Marwan al-Shehhi and Hamza al-Ghamdi.[4]

Al-Shehhi was, according to the official narrative of 9/11, a major player in the attacks. He is said to have been a close friend of ringleader Atta for years, having stayed with him in Hamburg and having been involved in early plans for attacks on the U.S. He is said to have had a joint bank account with Atta and to have been seen with him on many occasions in the U.S. On 9/11 itself, not long after Atta allegedly piloted a plane into the North Tower of the World Trade Center, Al-Shehhi allegedly piloted a plane into the South Tower.[5]

The links between Gloria Irish, the two Hijackers, and the anthrax attacks were apparently first reported on October 14, 2001.[6] The story was carried prominently in many newspapers on October 15.[7] The *Washington Post's* Justin Blum was quick to say that his newspaper had interviewed Gloria Irish twice in September—but, of course, this was in relation to her connection to the Hijackers, not in relation to anthrax since the anthrax attacks were not public knowledge at that time.[8]

On the occasions when she was willing to give interviews, Gloria Irish acknowledged that she remembered al-Shehhi and al-Ghamdi well, having driven them around town for three weeks.[9] She told one investigator: "I mean, Marwan called me all the time."[10] She evidently liked al-Shehhi. "He was the only customer I ever had who called up to say he would be five minutes late."[11] Or, again: "They were calling a lot. Marwan would come in laughing saying, 'It's us again.'"[12] Her two customers were, apparently, untypical for her. "I had never met Arabs before, and there they were." "I wanted to tell them I was Jewish, but I didn't."[13]

But if Gloria Irish had some familiarity with the two Hijackers, she had much more familiarity with Robert Stevens. Mike Irish had known Stevens for 25 years. Gloria Irish had found Robert Stevens' house for him.[14] That is to say, *she was the real estate agent of the first anthrax victim and of two of the 9/11 Hijackers.*

There were more than two Hijackers involved in the Irish affair. Nawaf al-Hazmi was said to have accompanied his two fellow Hijackers, as well as Irish, on their search for housing.[15] And once the two apartments were found, two Hijackers settled down in each one, making the apartments found by Irish home to four Hijackers.[16] The Delray Racquet Club apartment at 755 Dotterel Road, one of the two apartments, was a site of serious federal investigation. According to an October 15, 2001 article by the *St. Petersburg Times*:[17]

> The Delray apartment is central to a massive federal investigation into the terrorist attacks. Investigators trying to piece the puzzle together created a diagram that includes photos of the 19 hijackers who seized control of four airplanes on Sept. 11.
>
> At the center of the diagram, which was obtained by the *Miami Herald*: an image of a house with the address 755 Dotterel Road. Arrows connect nine of the hijackers to the icon.

The *St. Petersburg Times* posed the question: "It is clear that the apartment was a meeting ground for terrorists, authorities say. Now they must determine whether unit 1504 was also a hatching ground for the anthrax attacks."[18]

The *St. Petersburg Times* had no hesitation in saying that these discoveries revealed a link between the Hijackers and the company, American Media Inc. (AMI), whose employee had died. The newspaper entitled its article, "Hijackers linked to tabloid," and it referred to "a clear link between the terrorists targeting America and the South Florida company hit by anthrax cases."[19] In truth, it was not merely the company that was linked: the physical building in Boca Raton that housed AMI was contaminated by anthrax spores. By the time the Gloria Irish connection was revealed three people in that building had tested positive for anthrax exposure and one of them (Robert Stevens) had developed inhalation anthrax and died.[20]

Gloria and Mike Irish tried to extricate themselves from this web of connections by promoting a coincidence theory. "I can't blame [the media] for trying to build a story, but in fact there was none," Gloria Irish is quoted as saying, while her husband, Mike, added: "It was just a total coincidence."[21]

The Irishes are not the only ones committed to the coincidence theory. When the FBI first publicly spoke of Gloria Irish in relation to anthrax (on October 14, 2001), the Bureau simultaneously implied it had discovered a connection between the Hijackers and the anthrax case and that this connection was only apparent. "It's just a coincidence right now," said FBI spokesperson Judy Orihuela.[22] The *Washington Post* explained that, according to Orihuela, "there is no indication that Gloria Irish's work with the suspected hijackers is connected to the anthrax case."[23] Although Orihuela said hopefully that, "I'm sure there will be some sort of follow-up,"[24] the coincidence theory remains to this day the FBI's choice.

But the coincidence theory is not credible. In addition to other links to be explored in this chapter, there are obvious facts about the spatial congruence just explored that cannot be ignored. Many Hijackers lived, at one time or another, in this vicinity. "Six of them had addresses in Delray Beach or Fort Lauderdale, a few miles from the AMI building where the *Sun* was published."[25] AMI employees are said to have gone to the same gym as Atta.[26] In addition, two of the Hijackers were reported to have taken out subscriptions to publications of AMI, where Stevens worked.[27] Mike Irish, a licensed pilot, was a former member of the Civil Air Patrol based at Lantana airport, the same airport where Atta supposedly rented a plane in August, 2001.[28]Anthrax victim Stevens lived in Lantana.[29]

Academic researchers have largely tended to dismiss the Florida connections by accepting the FBI's coincidence theory. Jeanne Guillemen comments in her 2011 study:

> Bureau agents had put enormous energy into testing the terrorists' cars, personal possessions, and apartments for any signs of *B. anthracis* and found nothing. Coincidences abounded in Florida—al Qaeda operatives had rented an apartment through a real estate agent married to the editor of *The Sun*—but no evidence of a foreign source for the letters had surfaced.[30]

The question, however, is not whether actual hijackers were involved in sending out letters laden with anthrax spores: the question is whether fictions, verbal or enacted, were intentionally created to make this narrative seem credible. The Hijackers did not have anthrax, but the script portrayed them as likely to have it.

Some sought a way to rescue the FBI's feeble coincidence hypothesis, explaining the Florida connection by assuming that Ivins, or a similar lone wolf, was an opportunistic killer whom September 11, 2001 had motivated to frame Muslims and fraudulently construct a link to 9/11, making a first attempt in Florida because Florida by that time was already well known as a haunt of the Hijackers.

A theory of this sort was put forth pretty early in the investigation (before Ivins was a person of interest) by Don Foster, a professor of English whom the FBI had brought into the investigation.[31] Foster suggested that the anthrax killer may have been a misguided American scientist with access to highly lethal anthrax. This scientist, having seen the devastation of the 9/11 attacks and knowing how vulnerable the U.S. was to a bioweapons attack, might have wanted to make the point that the U.S. needed to start large scale funding of bioweapons research and thought the point could be made in a dramatic way with a few casualties. In order to link the attack to 9/11 and thus keep attention focused on foreign terrorists he or she chose Florida, where the hijackers were known to have based themselves, as the obvious choice for an initial attack.

Foster's theory will not fly without major reworking. In addition to the weaknesses of any lone wolf theory, which this book sets forth, Foster's explanation, while it might explain why anthrax was delivered to Florida, will have difficulty explaining the precise and multiple connections between the Hijackers and AMI. The full set of connections between Stevens, Gloria Irish, AMI, and the Hijackers was not made public until after Robert Stevens' death.[32] A Bruce Ivins or similar anthrax scientist would not have had access to this detailed information in time to target the first victim. Moreover, all evidence that indicates that the master narrative of the fall attacks had been established prior to 9/11—inter alia setting up Iraq through false statements about its anthrax supplies and means of delivery—rules out opportunistic patriots. The evidence suggests a grand plan, not an opportunistic foray.

The Florida narratives referred to above do not exhaust the repertoire of stories meant to connect the purported al-Qaeda attackers to the anthrax attacks. In addition to the crop-duster scenarios discussed later in this chapter, *The New York Times* published a story of a Hijacker with a mysterious black lesion on his leg, later judged by some experts to have been cutaneous anthrax.[33] (The chief experts in this case were associated with the Johns Hopkins Center for Civilian Biodefense, one of the co-sponsors of the Dark Winter simulation.[34]) The same article reported a Hijacker looking for relief from irritation of the hands, supposedly resulting from his work with chemicals needed for the production of bioweapons.[35] There was a report of Hijacker corporeal remains, after the alleged crash of United Airlines Flight 93 on 9/11, testing positive for anthrax,[36] and a separate report of an al-Qaeda facility in an "overseas site" that tested positive for anthrax.[37]

All of these reports were used to link the 9/11 attacks to the anthrax attacks. Considered important evidence at one time, the reports are now passed over in silence.

The Hijackers

Readers unfamiliar with dissident writings questioning the official version of the events of 9/11 may find this book's skeptical treatment of the Hijackers surprising and perplexing. Why are some people not convinced that these men hijacked planes on 9/11? And if they did not hijack planes does this mean that they had no connection to 9/11 and that their presence in the anthrax narratives fails to connect the anthrax attacks to the 9/11 attacks?

Although there are numerous uncertainties about their identities and histories, there was certainly a group of young Arab men with connections to the 9/11 operation. There is a wealth of material relating to their presence in the U.S. prior to the attacks—renting apartments, attending flight schools—and to their suspicious actions during the immediate lead-up to the attacks.[38] But there is no credible evidence that they were involved in planning the attacks and there is no credible evidence they hijacked four planes on September 11. Rather, they appear to have been following a script, laying a trail that would later lead people to conclude they were hijackers. What their awareness of the overall operation may have been it is difficult to say.

The following remarks are aimed at providing a brief introduction to the skeptical stance toward the Hijackers.

Burden of proof

The concept of burden of proof suggests that if someone is accused of a crime the responsibility of providing evidence and making a case lies with the accusers. The accused, and those supporting the accused, do not have an equivalent responsibility to prove innocence. The accused is to be presumed innocent.

If the U.S. government is convinced the 19 Arab men carried out the crime it must present its evidence. Indeed, this was the request of the Taliban, who indicated they would then turn over Osama bin Laden (thus obviating what would become the longest war in U.S. history)—but such proof was never forthcoming. The exhortation to simply trust the U.S. government, and the studies and reports associated with that government (such as the *9/11 Commission Report* and the various studies by the Federal Emergency Management Agency and the National Institute of Standards and Technology), is misguided. Deciding to trust government and to ignore evidence that conflicts with what government claims is unwise at the best of times, and in the present case it is strikingly irrational. The government that accused these 19 men of carrying out hijackings is the same government that made false statements about Iraq 935 times; it is the same government that is revealed in the Downing Street memo and in much other documentation as having conspired to deceive the public in order to carry out its agenda.

The U.S. government's attempts to furnish evidence that the 19 Arab men hijacked planes on 9/11 have failed to meet basic standards.

Researcher Elias Davidsson has noted that, "the following five classes of evidence should have been produced by the US authorities in September 2001 or shortly thereafter:" [39]

1. *Authenticated* passenger lists (or flight

manifests), listing the names of all the passengers and crew members, including those suspected of hijacking;
2. *Authenticated* boarding cards (or their detached coupons), on which the names of all the passengers and crew members figure, including those suspected of hijacking;
3. *Authenticated* security videos from the airports, which depict the passengers (and the alleged hijackers) arriving at the airport, in front of check-in counters, passing security checkpoints and boarding the aircraft;
4. *Sworn testimonies* of personnel who attended the boarding of the aircraft;
5. Formal identification of the bodies or bodily remains from the crash sites, including *chain-of-custody reports*."

U.S. authorities, Davidsson notes, have not only failed to deliver all five of these classes of evidence but have failed to deliver a single one.

But the FBI's case concerning the 9/11 attacks is not merely unproved: it has a host of difficulties that make it extremely implausible. Here are eight categories under which these difficulties can be organized.

1. Strange behavior of the Hijackers

The 9/11 Commission Report makes inadequate distinctions when dealing with the religious beliefs and practices of the Hijackers. One moment we receive evidence that they were pious Muslims; the next minute we are supposed to believe they were "fundamentalist;" and then we are led to believe they were violent extremists keen to kill themselves and large numbers of innocent others.[40] Further, *The 9/11 Commission Report* does not attempt to deal adequately with the media reports, which began soon after 9/11, of the peculiar behavior of the Hijackers, which included consumption of alcohol to the point of intoxication, as well as indulgence in cocaine, prostitutes, sex toys and lap-dancing.[41] This behavior certainly is not compatible with the first two options (piety and fundamentalism), and, in fact, stands as evidence that these characterizations were false.

The questions must be asked: Who were these men, and what were their real beliefs and aims?

2. Anomalies in the behavior of people on the hijacked planes

Pilots whose planes are being hijacked can punch in a hijack code to let the Federal Aviation Administration (FAA) know what is happening. It takes a few seconds to enter this four-digit code. Yet, although we are told four planes were hijacked on 9/11, not one of the eight men trained to do this (four pilots and four copilots) entered the code. In the case of "Flight 93," which allegedly crashed in Shanksville after a passenger revolt, we are told it took more than 30 seconds for the Hijackers to break through the door and overwhelm the pilot and copilot, yet no hijack code was entered.[42]

Within this category of anomalies belong the stories of passengers on the hijacked flights making phone calls, including cell phone calls, describing their situation and sending messages to loved ones. The contradictions, peculiarities and impossibilities in these phone calls have been catalogued and are available for public review.[43]

3. "Drama queen" episodes

This category includes those cases where a Hijacker

for whom secrecy is crucial repeatedly draws attention to himself, laying down a trail while creating an unforgettable persona.

Here is a partial list of Mohamed Atta stories and episodes:

a. Atta Annoys Airport Employees[44]
b. Atta Leaves Incriminating Evidence in his Luggage (below, point 5)
c. Atta is Bitten By a Dog[45]
d. Atta Visits a Drugstore and Frightens an Employee[46]
e. Atta Gets Pulled Over for Driving Without a License (and has a warrant for his arrest issued after he fails to show up for his court hearing)[47]
f. Atta Abandons a Stalled Plane on the Runway[48]
g. Atta Seeks a Federal Loan to Help Him Commit Mass Murder (later in this chapter)
h. Atta Gets Drunk and Swears at a Restaurant Employee[49]
i. Atta Threatens to Cut the Throat of a Federal Employee (later in this chapter)

In at least two of these episodes (c, e) Atta's actions apparently brought him to the attention of the police, and in two other cases (a, d) he appears to have narrowly missed the attention of the police. This seems like odd behavior for the ringleader of a secret operation.

Atta did not necessarily do all the things recounted in these tales. As pointed out in this book, we often find ourselves confronting fiction of various sorts. But whether the accounts were accurate or fictional, they had the effect of making the Mohamed Atta persona frightening and unforgettable. And after a certain point a conflict arises between this persona and the profile fitting a sophisticated leader on a secret mission.

4. Inability to carry out duties

The skills, determination and physical robustness of the men who hijacked four airplanes on 9/11—subduing crews and passengers and piloting the planes to new and very precise destinations—would have needed to be exceptional. But the evidence we have of the official Hijackers does not support this characterization.

Hani Hanjour exemplifies the point.[50]

Hanjour was, according to the official story of 9/11, the man who piloted a Boeing 757 into the Pentagon. The act was described at the time as a very impressive feat of flying.[51] While Hanjour could have simply steered the plane into the very large roof of the Pentagon, hoping for the best—there would have been many casualties—he is said to have chosen instead to execute a rapid and precise spiral descent so as to come in low and strike the side of the building virtually at ground level, clipping light poles as he went.[52]

ABC News was told by an air traffic controller at Dulles International Airport: "The speed, the maneuverability, the way that he turned, we all thought in the radar room, all of us experienced air traffic controllers, that that was a military plane."[53]

Who was this man, described by the 9/11 Commission as "the operation's most experienced pilot"[54]? Hanjour has been characterized by those who met him in one of the many flight schools he attended as small, unassuming and quiet, and as *an extraordinarily poor pilot*.[55] One of his flight instructors said: "He could not fly at all."[56]

On what did the 9/11 Commission base its claim that Hanjour had the competence to fly a Boeing 757 the way it was allegedly flown on 9/11? The Report notes that he had obtained a private pilot's license in the late 1990s, and that he followed this up with "a commercial pilot certificate" in 1999.[57] There are numerous elements of the story, however, that the Report omitted. It omitted the mystery as to when and where he received his "commercial pilot certificate"—the

FAA refused to say.[58] Moreover, as Jeremy Hammond has pointed out, "[c]ontrary to the...assertion that this certificate allowed him 'to fly commercial jets,' in fact it only allowed him to begin passenger jet training. Hanjour did so, only to fail the class."[59]

The Commission Report also neglected to note that Hanjour had been reported repeatedly to the FAA by one of his flight schools, Jet Tech, whose manager, Peggy Chevrette, found his skills completely inadequate.[60]

While admitting that his skills were substandard,[61] the 9/11 Commission suggested that perseverance eventually led him to master the art of flying.[62] The evidence overwhelmingly suggests that this is false. He never mastered the art. Just three weeks prior to the 9/11 operation, Hanjour was still unable to handle competently a single-engine Cessna.[63] As for his competence in handling a Boeing 757, there is no evidence that he had ever flown any sort of jet.[64]

The Commission's claim that Hanjour's perseverance had finally paid off and that he had attained, in the weeks before 9/11, the required skills, seemed to receive support from an assessment Hanjour received shortly before the 9/11 attacks. In an endnote dealing with August, 2001 preparations for the 9/11 attacks, the Commission Report notes that "Hanjour successfully conducted a challenging certification flight supervised by an instructor at Congressional Air Charters of Gaithersburg, Maryland, landing at a small airport with a difficult approach. The instructor thought Hanjour may have had training from a military pilot because he used a terrain recognition system for navigation." The endnote indicates its source as "Eddie Shalev interview (Apr. 9, 2004)."[65]

The FBI interview of Eddie Shalev was finally released in 2009.[66] In this document we learn that Shalev, who formerly "served in the Israeli [*sic*] Defense Forces in the paratroop regiment," came to the U.S. a few months before 9/11 (April, 2001), having been "sponsored for employment" by Congressional Air Charters. The document notes that Shalev was left unemployed when Congressional Air Charters went out of business and that he might soon (in 2004, it seems) have to go back to Israel.

Presumably, Shalev did go back to Israel: researchers trying to find him in the U.S. have been unsuccessful.[67]

Shalev's judgment conflicts with a mass of contrary testimony about Hanjour's flying skills. There is no valid reason to favor an assessment by a vanished man from a defunct company over assessments made by known, competent and accessible persons in the U.S. who trained and tested Hanjour and whose descriptions of his skills are a matter of record.

Not surprisingly, a number of pilots experienced in flying Boeing 757s and familiar with the details of the movements of the plane that approached the Pentagon on 9/11 have said that whoever or whatever may have been controlling the plane, it was not definitely not Hani Hanjour.[68]

The Hanjour case throws into question the entire Hijacker narrative.

5. Staged crime scenes

The Chinese have an expression that may be translated loosely as "painting legs on the snake." The expression is said to come from an old story about two artists.[69] The artists were rivals and decided on a competition to see who could paint the best snake in the shortest time. One artist finished so quickly that he had time to spare, and he decided to improve his snake by painting legs on it. Naturally, he lost the competition. He had gone too far and added false details that discredited his work.

There are several accounts of Hijackers where the creators of scenarios have painted legs on the snake. The story of Mohamed Atta asking for a government loan, recounted later in this chapter, is one such instance.

But in addition to narrative accounts we also confront

cases of physical evidence that appear to be legs on the snake. More familiar designations for what we face here are "planted evidence" and "staged crime scenes."

The passport of Hijacker Satam al-Suqami was allegedly found intact near the World Trade Center crime scene. A journalist writing for the *Guardian*, although wrongly identifying the Hijacker as Atta, was able to see the absurdity of this evidence: "the idea that Atta's passport had escaped from that inferno unsinged [strains] credulity."[70]

Another example of apparently planted evidence is the material supposedly left by Mohamed Atta at Logan airport. In the developed form of this tale, "flight simulation manuals for Boeing airplanes, a copy of the Koran, a religious cassette tape, a note to other hijackers about mental preparations, and Atta's will, passport, and international driver's license" were all found in the luggage that was, mysteriously, not loaded onto his final flight.[71] The suspect nature of the evidence did not escape the immediate notice of investigators. Seymour Hersh noted years ago:

> Many of the investigators believe that some of the initial clues that were uncovered about the terrorists' identities and preparations, such as flight manuals, were meant to be found. A former high-level intelligence official told me, "Whatever trail was left was left deliberately—for the FBI to chase."[72]

The question is: *who* deliberately left this trail? There was no evident advantage in such a procedure for either al-Qaeda or a state sponsor of al-Qaeda.

These examples are two of many that could be given—the Hijackers left a treasure trove of evidence.[73]

Those who refuse to believe that the U.S. military or intelligence community would plant evidence in such a serious case should consult the Operation Northwoods planning document of 1962, wherein the Joint Chiefs of Staff expressed the view that "[i]t is possible to create an incident which will make it appear that Communist MIGs have destroyed a USAF aircraft over international waters in an unprovoked attack". Disturbingly, the document outlines how evidence might then be planted, in the hope of finding, through such a fraudulent incident, a pretext to invade Cuba:

> At precisely the same time that the aircraft was presumably shot down a submarine or small surface craft would disburse F-101 parts, parachute, etc., at approximately 15 to 20 miles off the Cuban coast and depart... Search ships and aircraft could be dispatched and parts of aircraft found.[74]

6. Deception and cover-up

The many instances of deception that the Bush administration was involved in preceding the illegal invasion of Iraq are well known. Recall the 935 false statements referred to earlier. But some of the known fictions involved the Hijackers. The "Mohamed Atta Visits Prague" story is a case in point: as noted earlier, this fiction was promoted by several members of the Bush administration and had a clear central purpose of tying Iraq to the Hijackers. But there is plenty of evidence of deception also on the part of the official investigating bodies charged with looking into the 9/11 attacks in addition to that related to Hani Hanjour, described above. David Ray Griffin's book, *The 9/11 Commission Report: Omissions and Distortions*,[75] gives numerous examples.

Once these deceptions come to light we are forced to ask: Why omit and distort if there is nothing to hide? Why pretend Hani Hanjour flew into the Pentagon? Why pretend Satam al-Suqami's passport was found at the World Trade Center?

Those who deliberately misrepresent evidence of a crime make themselves suspects in the crime.

7. Intelligence connections

Early reports after 9/11 noted that some of the Hijackers had spent time in San Diego. The *San Diego Union-Tribune* gave details on September 16, 2001, noting:[76]

> Agents from the FBI and the Bureau of Alcohol, Tobacco and Firearms Friday night sifted through belongings left behind by Nawaf Alhamzi and Khalid Al-Midhar, who rented a room from September through December last year [2000] in the Lemon Grove home of prominent Muslim leader Abdussattar Shaikh.

Elaborating on the nature of the San Diego host, the *Union-Tribune* explained: "The retired San Diego State University English professor said he often invites students to live in his five-bedroom house for companionship and to learn other cultures and languages."

Shaikh, who had "deep ties to San Diego," was said to have become "fond of Alhamzi". (Recall that Nawaf al-Hazmi, also known as Alhamzi, apparently accompanied Irish, al-Shehhi and al-Ghamdi on their later apartment hunting in Florida.) Outraged "after hearing his former house guests identified as terrorists in a radio news report," Shaikh contacted the FBI.

Exactly one year later, September 16, 2002, the American public discovered how easy it must have been for Shaikh to contact the FBI. He had been a trusted FBI asset for years. "The connection just discovered by congressional investigators," said *Newsweek,* "has stunned some top counterterrorism officials."[77]

Neither the officials nor the media seem to have remained stunned for long, apparently accepting the theory that the odd circumstance was simply a result of poor communication. The FBI did not allow Shaikh to testify before the 9/11 Congressional inquiry.[78]

This was not the only case of Hijacker connections to intelligence agencies. For example, it eventually came out that one of the Hijackers, Ziad Jarrah, had three cousins alleged to have worked for intelligence agencies. One had worked for East German, West German and Libyan intelligence,[79] while the other two were arrested in Lebanon in 2008 and accused of spying for Israel.[80] Possible connections between the Hijackers and Israeli intelligence are especially interesting.

A leaked 2001 document from the Drug Enforcement Administration (DEA), an agency of the Department of Justice, made it clear that over 120 Israeli intelligence personnel, pretending to be art students, were aggressively active in the U.S. during 2000 and 2001, in the same places as the Hijackers.[81]

Journalist Christopher Ketcham set out many of the key facts about the "art students" in 2002[82] and added further information in a 2007 article in *CounterPunch*.[83] In the latter article he also discussed a set of Israeli intelligence agents associated with Urban Moving Systems in New York City.

About the "art students," Ketcham remarks:

> In retrospect, the fact that a large number of "art students" operated out of Hollywood [within the 71 mile strip of territory mentioned above] is intriguing, to say the least. During 2001, the city, just north of Miami, was a hotbed of al-Qaeda activity and served as one of the chief staging grounds for the hijacking of the World Trade Center planes and Pennsylvania plane; it was home to fifteen of the nineteen future hijackers, nine in Hollywood and six in the surrounding area. Among the 120 suspected Israeli spies posing as art students, more than thirty lived in the

Hollywood area, ten in Hollywood proper.[84]

Ketcham gives an example of the spatial congruence at issue. Hanan Serfaty, an "art student" who was actually a former Israeli intelligence officer, "rented two apartments close to the mail drop and apartment of Mohammed Atta and four other hijackers." Atta and al-Shehhi lived "some 1,800 feet from Serfaty's South 21st Avenue apartment."[85]

Neither Ketcham nor the publications in which his articles appeared were prepared to consider the possibility that the Israeli spies may have been actively involved in some way in the 9/11 attacks, but disconcerting facts emerge from Ketcham's study and other sources.

The spatial congruence noted for Hollywood, Florida, for example, can hardly be a coincidence:

> In at least six urban centers, suspected Israeli spies and 9/11 hijackers and/or al-Qaeda-connected suspects lived and operated near one another, in some cases less than half a mile apart, for various periods during 2000-1 in the run-up to the attacks.[86]

In addition, there is strong evidence that Israeli intelligence operatives working with a front company in New York City, Urban Moving Systems, had detailed foreknowledge of the 9/11 attacks. The UMS operatives were caught celebrating, and catching the World Trade Center and each others' joyous expressions on camera, after the impact of the *first* plane into the World Trade Center, before the rest of the country had even reached the conclusion that a terrorist attack was taking place.[87]

Ketcham, and several others in the mainstream media who have examined this issue, have been concerned that the Israelis (those working with UMS as well as the "art students"), due to their spying on al-Qaeda operatives, may have gained detailed foreknowledge of the 9/11 attacks that they then did not share with U.S. intelligence agencies. Of course the other possibility is that the Israelis were directly complicit in the 9/11 operation.

It was claimed in the fall of 2001 that U.S. intelligence had been warned by Israel before 9/11 of a major upcoming attack in the U.S. by Bin Laden. The story of Israel's warnings was widely reported in the media. The warnings were said to have run from the summer until late August of 2001 and to have included considerable detail, such as the fact that it was an al-Qaeda operation, that there were 19 men involved, and that Iraq might be involved as well.[88]

But the actions of the UMS operatives are hard to reconcile with the theory of the benign Israelis spies. Their early and joyous celebrations suggest that, instead of dedicating themselves to giving actionable warnings that could have led to the saving of lives, they were happy the attacks were successful.

8. Revised narratives

Sufficient documentation has survived to allow us to see fictional Hijacker narratives in the process of construction. We can see the false starts, the contradictions and unsupported allegations, the revisions and the cover-ups. It is impossible to take these stories at face value once the cutting and pasting have been made visible.

Some of the stitched together stories are very important. An example is the story of the Hijackers (originally Adnan and Ameer Bukhari, later revised to Mohamed Atta and Abdul Aziz al-Omari) who flew from Portland, Maine to Boston on the morning of 9/11, thereafter joining the two doomed flights out of Boston. (One of the significant elements of this tale is Atta's luggage, referred to earlier, which failed to make it from his Portland flight to his Boston flight.) To support the revised version of this story the FBI eventually offered a detailed chronology with photographs and videos, as well as an affidavit.[89] But this evidence is riddled with contradictions, leaving the story without support.[90]

When the chief of the local Portland police attempted to investigate these incidents he was told by the FBI to mind his own business. In fact, he was told he was risking "obstruction of justice."[91] The FBI had been granted exclusive control over the investigation of the 9/11 events, and there were many instances of local police throughout the country being ignored or pushed aside.[92]

The above are classes of evidence that do not fit the official narrative of the Hijackers and that, therefore, force sincere investigators to doubt whether the 19 Arab men really hijacked planes on 9/11. If they did not hijack planes, some party went to a great deal of trouble to pretend that they did.

Crop-duster Planes

How did the media and the government explain the foreknowledge of the anthrax attacks once the actual attacks began? Surely with a run on Cipro and a whole series of warnings and representations related to imminent bioweapons attacks there must have been some evidential basis—some troublesome event or events—that could be used to justify this foreknowledge.

There had been urgent but vague references to the dangers of biological and chemical weapons immediately after the 9/11 plane attacks and, as has been indicated earlier, these continued until the anthrax attacks began. There was also a proliferation of written materials and of dramatic fiction about bioweapons attacks in the year or two prior to the attacks of the fall of 2001. But the most concrete and sustained set of evidential claims involved an apparent connection between the 9/11 Hijackers and crop-duster planes.

On at least two occasions (September 16 and September 23-24) in the interim between 9/11 and the anthrax attacks all 3500-4000 crop-duster planes in the U.S. were grounded by the FAA. These developments were related to several reported events.

The main post-9/11 crop-duster warnings began on September 22, 2001. An article written for *TIME Magazine* announced on September 22 that the September 16 grounding of the planes was caused by the fact that "U.S. law enforcement officials have found a manual on the operation of cropdusting equipment while searching terrorist hideouts."[93] The authors went on to explain:

> The discovery has added to concerns among government counterterrorism experts that the bin Laden conspirators may have been planning—or may still be planning—to disperse biological or chemical agents from a cropdusting plane normally used for agricultural purposes.

They added that, according to "sources," the materials in question were found among the belongings of Zacarias Moussaoui.

After September 11 Moussaoui was considered to have been a member of the Hijacker group. He was given the epithet, "the 20th hijacker." We were apparently supposed to believe when the *TIME* article appeared, that because he had been interested in crop-dusters the rest of this dangerous team was also interested in crop-dusters.

Other media also mentioned on September 22 the growing concern about crop-dusters. The *Washington Post*, for example, noted that "the FBI asked operators of the nation's 3,500 crop-duster planes to be on the lookout for suspicious behavior around their hangars."[94] The authors of the article expressed concern about "a cloud of microbes released from a small plane" and put this worry within the wider context of worries that a biological attack may already be in progress and that the physical signs may simply not have been recognized yet. Rick Weiss, author of the *Post* article, noted that in the previous week, "a National Guard unit with special training in bioterrorism was mobilized, as was a team with similar expertise from the federal Centers for Disease Control and Prevention in Atlanta."

The second piece of information, apparently responsible for the September 23-24 grounding of crop-dusters, appeared to be more significant. Information was released to the effect that between February and September, 2001, groups of "Middle Eastern men" had visited a municipal airport in Belle Glade, Florida—"about an hour's drive from Delray Beach, the coastal community where some of the alleged hijackers are believed to have lived"—to inspect and enquire about crop-dusters.[95] Willie Lee, "general manager of South Florida Crop Care," said the men described themselves as flight students.[96] The apparent leader of the group, identified by employee James Lester as Mohamed Atta,[97] was aggressive.

> "I recognized him because he stayed on my feet all the time. I just about had to push him away from me," Lester said.
>
> Lee said the men pestered employees with 'odd questions' about his 502 Air Tractor crop-duster. He said they asked about the range of the airplane, how much it could haul in chemicals, how difficult it was to fly, and how much fuel it could carry.
>
> During one visit, they followed Lester around, asking questions while he was working on one of the planes. Another time, they carried video equipment and asked to photograph the inside of the cockpit.[98]

Atta supposedly visited twice more over the following months, while a variety of other Middle Eastern men came back repeatedly for further details. The visitors took more photographs and video footage of the planes. At one point they wanted to enter the cockpit, but Lester refused to allow this.[99]

Willie Lee confirmed that the "groups of two or three Middle Eastern men came by nearly every weekend for six or eight weeks prior to the Sept. 11 terrorist attacks—including the weekend [Saturday, September 8] just prior to the assaults."[100] Lee estimated that, all told, perhaps 12 to 15 men had been involved over time and that each visit typically lasted 45-60 minutes. He added that, "They were asking the types of questions that other people didn't ask," and that they were so persistent and annoying that he asked the "Belle Glade Police Department to run them off"—without success.[101]

On the same day the media reported this information, September 24, 2001, Attorney General John Ashcroft testified before Congress.[102] After explaining that crop-dusters could be used to "distribute chemical or biological weapons of mass destruction," he stated that Mohamed Atta, the supposed ringleader of the "hijackers," "had been compiling information about crop-dusting before the Sept. 11 attacks."

The following day there was a shocking new development: Mohamed Atta had "apparently walked into a U.S. Department of Agriculture office in Florida last year [2000] and asked about a loan to buy a crop-duster plane."[103] This information, uncovered for the first time on September 24, readers were told, "has heightened fears that the United States may be at risk of an aerial assault involving biological or chemical weapons." Further details were scarce at this time because the key witness, Johnelle Bryant, "was told by authorities not to speak about it." Fortunately, ABC News was able to fill out the narrative in 2002—the story will be discussed later in this chapter.

In the meantime, in the days and weeks following these early reports, well into the period of the growing panic and the deaths from anthrax, crop-dusters became a staple in the news media, being referred to repeatedly in articles that associated the Hijackers with the anthrax attacks. For example, on October 10, Mohammad Akhter, at the time executive director of the American Public Health Association and former commissioner of public health for the District of Columbia, began an article on bioterrorism with the sentence: "The disclosure that terrorists may have been interested in using crop-dusting planes to spread any number of deadly diseases shows how close we may be to getting our first real dose of bioterrorism."[104]

Perhaps the high point in the crop-dusters' fame came on October 11, the day after Akhter's article appeared, when George W. Bush included in a public address about the war on terror the following remarks:

> ...let me give you one example of a specific threat we received. You may remember recently there was a lot of discussion about crop-dusters. We received knowledge that perhaps an al Qaeda operative was prepared to use a crop-duster to spray a biological weapon or a chemical weapon on American people, and so we responded. We contacted every crop-dust location, airports from which crop-dusters leave. We notified crop-duster manufacturers to a potential threat. We knew full well that in order for a crop-duster to become a weapon of mass destruction would require a retrofitting, and so we talked to machine shops around where crop-dusters are located.
>
> We took strong and appropriate action, and we will do so anytime we receive a credible threat.[105]

In the question period after his speech Bush was asked what one was supposed to do, concretely, when told by intelligence agencies to increase one's awareness or to be on the lookout for something suspicious. His response must have caused people on the streets of New York and Washington to scratch their heads in puzzlement: "You know, if you find a person that you've never seen before getting in a crop-duster that doesn't belong to you, report it."

The crop-duster accounts, or at least those coming from Belle Glade, do appear to have been based on actual incidents involving real people. Independent researchers assert that they have confirmed that the Middle Eastern men in question were not only interested in the crop-dusters but were intrusive and impolite, making themselves unwelcome and unforgettable.[106]

But why were crop-dusters such a concern and what were they supposed to signify?

The idea of mounting an attack via planes with tanks full of biomaterial and nozzles for aerial dispersal above the target has been around for quite a long time. The U.S. had developed its own method of doing this between the mid-1950s and the early 1960s.[107] Miller *et al* claim that evidence gathered throughout the 1990s suggested that Iraq was pushing ahead not only with the production of large quantities of sophisticated anthrax but also with the development of crop-dusters or similar planes as a means of delivering the anthrax.[108]

These authors are not the only ones to have made such claims about Iraq. In a list of developments in the Iraqi bioweapons program during the 1990s, the Monterey Institute of International Studies of Middlebury College prepared an "Iraq Biological Chronology" in which crop-dusters were listed in 1997 and 1998 as potential delivery vehicles being developed by Iraq.[109]

Occasionally these claims made it to the mainstream media. In 1997 a story appeared about Iraq's alleged crop-dusters and the danger they represented. The *Deseret News* had an article entitled, "Could Iraq spread death via remote crop dusters?"[110] The source of this story, says the *Deseret News*, is *The Sunday Times* and, ultimately, "Iraqi and Western intelligence sources." In the article we learn of Iraq's anthrax and of "Iraqi President Saddam Hussein's determination to hang on to the crop-duster system, which [*The Sunday Times*] said he calls his 'doomsday option'."

What are we to say, then, about the crop-duster stories that led to the run on Cipro and the widespread feeling, in September of 2001, that an anthrax attack on the U.S. was about to take place? The beginning of an answer can be achieved by looking in more detail at the story of Mohamed Atta Seeking a Loan.

As mentioned above, the story appeared in rudimentary form on September 25, 2001.[111] ABC News gave a full version of the story on June 6, 2002.[112] Brian Ross interviewed the key witness, Johnelle Bryant.

Just prior to the Johnelle Bryant incident, Mohamed Atta had been, according to *The Observer* (September 30, 2001), in Europe:

> [Atta] was under surveillance between January and May last year [2000] after he was reportedly observed buying large quantities of chemicals in Frankfurt, apparently for the production of explosives and for biological warfare. The US agents reported to have trailed Atta are said to have failed to inform the German authorities about their investigation.[113]

Directly after these Frankfurt activities Atta attempted to acquire, in the United States, a plane that could be used for crop-dusting. Presumably still being tracked by U.S. agents, he made his way to Florida, and it was here that he was interviewed by Johnelle Bryant, a manager at an agency of the U.S. Department of Agriculture.

Bryant supposedly told authorities of her experience a few days after 9/11 when she recognized Atta's photograph in the newspaper. The authorities, after she allegedly passed a polygraph test, were said to have advised her not to talk about her experience.[114]

The function of Bryant's agency, she explained in her 2002 interview with Ross, was to make loans to farmers who were finding it impossible to obtain credit. Mohamed Atta entered her office seeking funds in late April or early May of 2000. (Although Bryant recalled a great many details of this encounter, she presumably did not take notes of the meeting, because she was unsure of the date.) Atta said he was from Egypt, via Afghanistan. He told Bryant his name, Mohamed Atta, and made sure she knew how to spell it. He was new to the U.S., he said, and wanted to fulfill his dream to fly planes, including crop-dusters. To this end he sought a loan of $650,000 with which to buy a two-engine, six-passenger aircraft. He wanted to modify the plane from its original form so that it could hold a very large chemical tank. He would then "run the spray nozzles along the wing span." With this extra capacity tank, he explained, he would be able to do all the spraying required in one flight, not needing to land to refill his tank as he would have to in an ordinary crop-duster. Bryant was confused by this requirement. She was also dubious about his plan, because she had some experience with crop-dusters and knew it was essential that they be small and agile. She expressed her doubts about his plan but he assured her that he was an engineer and could manage the modifications without any problem.

When Bryant explained to Atta that he could not simply walk out of her office with $650,000 in cash but would have to go through an application process, he became agitated. Noting the lack of security in the building, he asked what would stop him from going around her desk, cutting her throat, and taking the money from the large safe in the office. Bryant, unfazed, replied that they did not keep large amounts of cash in the safe and that, in any case, she knew karate. She went on to explain that he was ineligible for the loan because he was not a U.S. citizen.

Atta then noticed a picture on her wall. It was an aerial photograph of Washington, D.C. He became obsessed with the photograph and threw down cash on her desk, wanting to buy it. It was one of the best photos of Washington he had ever seen. He admired the view of the monuments and buildings of the city and paid special attention to the White House and the Capitol, as well as to the Pentagon, which he was able to point out. She refused to sell the photograph, which she said was a gift, but he continued the conversation by explaining that he wanted to visit Washington. He asked Bryant what the security was like in the various buildings there and whether he would be admitted.

Atta then said he would like to visit the World Trade Center in New York City. Again, he asked Bryant what the security was like. He also inserted into the conversation what seems to have been a recruitment probe. His organization, he explained, could use someone with insider knowledge of Washington, where Bryant had previously worked. Growing emotional, he told her the name of an organization, al-Qaeda, which he said was based in his country (she was not sure whether he meant Egypt or Afghanistan) and with which, he implied, he was associated. He next spoke of Osama bin Laden, telling Bryant Bin Laden "would someday be known as the world's greatest leader."

Bryant had never heard of either al-Qaeda or Osama bin Laden, but she wished Atta luck and pointed him to a bank where he might pursue his loan.

And that is the story of how a terrorist leader engaged in a top-secret operation sought a government loan to help him with his plan.

Are we really supposed to believe that the leader

of a group of men soon to successfully carry out one of the most lethal crimes in U.S. history would, a year before the operation, threaten to cut the throat of his interviewer—and do so in the context of pursuing his search for a plane with a large tank that would carry out its task on a single mission? That he would express interest in a view of Washington from the air? That he would also express interest in the World Trade Center and its security? That he would make sure his interlocutor knew his name and of his association with al-Qaeda and Osama Bin Laden? Are we to believe that he, evidently already being followed by U.S. agents suspecting him of planning an attack with biological or chemical weapons, sought hundreds of thousands of dollars from a U.S. government agency with which to acquire his delivery vehicle?

We confront two possibilities. The first possibility is that the story of Atta and the loan is pure fiction and the event never took place. Presumably, if this is the case someone coached Bryant. Who might this have been? What was the role of her interviewer, Brian Ross, known by the news website Gawker as "ABC News' Wrongest Reporter"?[115] Ross was certainly no stranger to fiction: he had taken the lead in the false bentonite stories meant to frame Iraq and he broke a number of misleading stories over the years that served the interests of the authors of the Global War on Terror.[116]

But suppose—this is option two—events unfolded as Bryant says. In this case Mohamed Atta was certainly no secretive al-Qaeda leader but a man laying down a trail we were supposed to follow. Other stories about him, some listed above in the discussion of the Hijackers, are similar. The man's task appears to have been to make himself unforgettable.

While it would be good to know which of these options is correct—whether we are dealing with verbal fiction (Bryant's) or enacted fiction (Atta's)—it is not actually necessary for us to figure this out. Either way, the event remains a fiction, constructed by some group to link the 9/11 and anthrax attacks while also establishing an evidential basis for the foreknowledge of the anthrax attacks.

Journalist Edward Jay Epstein has called the terror crop-dusters a "fictoid," a construction that was never grounded in reality but that entered into circulation, was promoted by the media, and was widely assumed to be true because it was referred to by multiple sources.[117] In this case the fictoid was deliberately manufactured for an ambitious propaganda campaign.

History professor Philipp Sarasin said some years ago:

> What can be said is that objectively, the cropduster announcement was so absurd as to border on disinformation. Anyone with so much liquid anthrax that they can conceive of using a cropduster to spread it is planning a terror attack whose dimensions dwarf the operational details of 9/11. Gallons of liquid anthrax presupposes [*sic*] large-scale industrial production capacity, a ready supply of money, and very carefully thought out high-tech transport logistics. Nobody has ever claimed that terrorists of whatever stripe have such resources to draw on. A person or group capable of planning bioterror of this magnitude does not have to search for cropduster manuals over the Internet or sound out mechanics on the subject of spraytank capacity.[118]

Sarasin's remarks are very insightful. They may, however, be qualified in two ways. First, the crop-duster narratives did not *border on* disinformation: they *were* disinformation. This is easier to recognize today than it was when Sarasin made his comments almost ten years ago. Second, it is not quite accurate to say that, "Nobody has ever claimed that terrorists...have such resources to draw on."

In the year 2000, Michael Osterholm, epidemiologist and bioterrorism expert, authored, with the help of journalist John Schwartz, a book called, *Living Terrors: What America Needs to Know to Survive the Coming Bioterrorist Catastrophe*.[119] Each section of the book opens with a fictional scenario, and one of these scenarios has a disillusioned former military scientist, Ed, working by himself in a basement laboratory. Ed, after solving various production problems, loads up his crop-duster plane and, having previously mastered the pilot's art, heads off to disperse his homegrown supply of anthrax above a packed sport stadium. The multi-skilled Ed is successful in killing a large number of people and producing social chaos.

Osterholm, if cornered, would probably admit that this scenario is not realistic. But the structure of the book, with its fictional interludes, allows him and his co-author to paint a picture—in this case of the lone wolf, and in another part of the book of the Double Perpetrator—that puts readers into a froth of apprehension. If challenged, the authors can always say: well, that part was just fiction!

Putting aside fictions, we are now in a position to draw conclusions about the crop-duster scenarios.

1. The crop-duster stories and/or incidents were meant to link the anthrax attacks to the 9/11 attacks. In this respect they are like the anthrax letters with "09-11-01" written at the top. The 9/11 Hijackers—Atta and his companions—constitute the central, visible link between the two sets of events, and this link holds regardless of whether the crop-duster fictions were verbal or enacted.

2. Al-Qaeda operatives, working by themselves, would have had no use for crop-dusters. As Sarasin rightly points out, crop-dusters make sense as a way of dispersing anthrax *only if one has access to a massive quantity of anthrax*, far more than al-Qaeda could have produced, even if the group had mastered the basic science. A state supplier is indicated.

Given the attempt, stretching over several years, to implicate Iraq in a crop-duster scenario, *it is clear that Iraq was the key target of this framing.*

3. Stories tying the Hijackers to Iraq, notably the tale, Mohamed Atta Visits Prague, surfaced at the same time as the crop-duster stories and were evidently meant to solidify this connection.

4. Although the foreknowledge of the anthrax attacks received an apparent evidential grounding in the crop-duster reports, this grounding was illusory because the crop-duster reports were disinformation.

5. It is clear why the crop-duster stories have fallen into obscurity and are now seldom mentioned, even though they were at one time pervasive. As long as the foreign group hypothesis was in play these stories were useful, but after the FBI admitted that the anthrax attacks were a domestic operation the stories had to be abandoned. *Given that the anthrax attacks were a domestic operation, and given that the Hijackers were implicated in that operation prior to its occurrence, the conclusion cannot be avoided: the 9/11 attacks were also a domestic operation.* This is the conclusion the FBI has been determined to avoid.

We cannot rule out the possibility that a crop-duster attack of some sort may actually have been planned at one time by those who laid down the trail to the Hijackers. In April, 2000 a military exercise involving a chemical attack in the U.S. using a crop-duster plane was held.[120]

The Powell Performance

The crop-duster tales were not a complete failure as a disinformation product. True, the reference to crop-dusters in the initial indictment of Moussaoui was later dropped,[121] but when Colin Powell made his infamous bogus presentation at the UN Security Council in the lead-up to the invasion of Iraq he did not hesitate to make reference to Iraq's dreaded aerial dispersion techniques.[122] Moreover, having assured those present that "every statement I make today is backed up by sources, solid sources," Powell held up a vial of simulated anthrax and said:

> My colleagues, when Iraq finally admitted having these weapons in 1995, the quantities were vast. Less than a teaspoon of dry anthrax, a little bit about this amount—this is just about the amount of a teaspoon—less than a teaspoon full of dry anthrax in an envelope shut down the United States Senate in the fall of 2001. This forced several hundred people to undergo emergency medical treatment and killed two postal workers just from an amount just about this quantity that was inside of an envelope.

This was classic propaganda. Powell did not claim Iraq was responsible for the attack on the Senate but he made sure Iraq, anthrax and the Senate were all mentioned together. He held the vial aloft for all to see. The fears of the fall of 2001 would have been instantly conjured up for Americans watching the performance.

Powell's presentation included more than misdirection, of course. It also included statements such as the following four that were simply false:

- In 2003 Iraq still possessed bioweapons and the capacity to produce more.
- Iraq had a long-range missile program that could be used to deliver its WMD.
- Iraq also possessed the means to disperse anthrax

from planes. (Powell showed a slide illustrating an Iraqi plane dispersing an anthrax simulant.)
- Iraq tolerated al Qaeda on its soil and was prepared to adopt a sponsor relationship to al Qaeda.

Actually, Iraq, a devastated and impoverished country when Powell gave his address in 2003, possessed no significant quantity of anthrax, nor had it possessed such since 1991 when it destroyed its stocks. By 1995-96 Iraq had destroyed even the technical infrastructure needed to reconstitute its bioweapons. In view of this, discussion of the technology required to deliver the non-existent anthrax was more or less irrelevant. Nonetheless, it is worth noting that Iraq's two main aerial dispersion devices for its anthrax—tanks with spray devices mounted on jets and aerosolizers for helicopters—were, as far as we can tell, minimally effective and did not, in any case, survive the 1991 Gulf War and Iraq's immediately subsequent destruction of its bioweapons material. The long-range missile program had also been terminated under pressure from UN inspectors and assorted intelligence officers—the UN inspection process was heavily infiltrated by intelligence agencies of countries hostile to Iraq—long before 2001-2003.[123]

Reference was made earlier in this book to the 935 false statements by the Bush administration with respect to Iraq. Powell's performance at the UN represents a peak in the graph of those statements. The U.S. Secretary of State displaying his vial of anthrax simulant before the international community just prior to a war of aggression against Iraq is one of the most telling gestures of the 21st century.

Endnotes

1 Christopher Ketcham, "What Did Israel Know in Advance of the 9/11 Attacks?," *CounterPunch*, 2007, 4, http://www.counterpunch.org/2007/03/07/what-did-israel-know-in-advance-of-the-9-11-at-

tacks/.

2 Thomas Tobin, "Florida: Terror's Launching Pad," *St. Petersburg Times*, September 1, 2002. This article includes a useful map.

3 A good introduction to this topic can be found in Cole, *The Anthrax Letters: A Bioterrorism Expert Investigates the Attacks That Shocked America*, pp. 34 ff. See also the History Commons timeline.

4 "History Commons: 2001 Anthrax Attacks," October 14, 2001: 'Strange Coincidence' Briefly Increases Suspicions Al-Qaeda is behind Anthrax Attacks.

5 *Wikipedia*, as of June, 2014, remains for most topics related to 9/11 a reliably uncritical repository of the official narrative. See, therefore, "Marwan Al-Shehhi," *Wikipedia*, accessed May 27, 2014, https://en.wikipedia.org/wiki/Marwan_al-Shehhi.

6 "History Commons: 2001 Anthrax Attacks," October 14, 2001: 'Strange Coincidence' Briefly Increases Suspicions Al-Qaeda is behind Anthrax Attacks.

7 Chris Tisch, "Hijackers Linked to Tabloid," *St. Petersburg Times*, October 15, 2001; Justin Blum, "Sun Editor's Wife Found Rentals for 2 Hijackers; FBI: Link May Be Just 'Coincidence,'" *The Washington Post*, October 15, 2001; Powell and Slevin, "Detective, Scientists Exposed to Anthrax; FBI Continues to Hunt for Letters' Origins"; Bill Egbert, "Fla. Paper Linked To Hijackers," *New York Daily News*, October 15, 2001; Alfonso Chardy, Wanda DeMarzo, and Ronnie Greene, "Tabloid Editor's Wife Rented Apartment to 2 Hijackers," *Miami Herald*, October 15, 2001.

8 Blum, "Sun Editor's Wife Found Rentals for 2 Hijackers; FBI: Link May Be Just 'Coincidence.'"

9 Frank Cerabino, "Encounters with 9/11 Hijackers Still Haunt Palm Beach County Residents," *The Palm Beach Post*, September 3, 2011.

10 Cole, *The Anthrax Letters: A Bioterrorism Expert Investigates the Attacks That Shocked America*.

11 Cerabino, "Encounters with 9/11 Hijackers Still Haunt Palm Beach County Residents."

12 Blum, "Sun Editor's Wife Found Rentals for 2 Hijackers; FBI: Link May Be Just 'Coincidence.'"

13 Cerabino, "Encounters with 9/11 Hijackers Still Haunt Palm Beach County Residents."

14 Cole, *The Anthrax Letters: A Bioterrorism Expert Investigates the Attacks That Shocked America*.

15 Cerabino, "Encounters with 9/11 Hijackers Still Haunt Palm Beach County Residents."

16 Ibid.

17 Tisch, "Hijackers Linked to Tabloid."

18 Ibid.

19 Ibid.

20 Blum, "Sun Editor's Wife Found Rentals for 2 Hijackers; FBI: Link May Be Just 'Coincidence.'"

21 Cole, *The Anthrax Letters: A Bioterrorism Expert Investigates the Attacks*

That Shocked America.

22 The FBI spokesperson, Judy Orihuela, is said to have told the media on October 14 that "there is now a link between the editor's wife and the terrorists," but she is then supposed to have added: "It's just a coincidence right now." "I'm sure there will be some sort of follow-up," she is quoted as adding hopefully. Tisch, "Hijackers Linked to Tabloid."

23 Blum, "Sun Editor's Wife Found Rentals for 2 Hijackers; FBI: Link May Be Just 'Coincidence.'"

24 Tisch, "Hijackers Linked to Tabloid."

25 Cole, *The Anthrax Letters: A Bioterrorism Expert Investigates the Attacks That Shocked America.*

26 See "AMI Employee says 'It was Terrorist Attack.'" Apparently published in the *Miami Herald*, Oct. 12, 2001, and archived here: http://www.freerepublic.com/focus/f-news/546427/posts

27 David Kidwell, Manny Garcia, and Larry Lebowitz, "Authorities Trace Anthrax That Killed Florida Man to Iowa Lab," *Knight Ridder/Tribune News Service*, October 9, 2001, http://www.accessmylibrary.com/coms2/summary_0286-6784004_ITM.

28 Tisch, "Hijackers Linked to Tabloid." See also the History Commons entry on Gloria Irish: http://www.historycommons.org/entity.jsp?entity=gloria_irish_1

29 Blum, "Sun Editor's Wife Found Rentals for 2 Hijackers; FBI: Link May Be Just 'Coincidence.'"

30 Guillemin, *American Anthrax: Fear, Crime, and the Investigation of the Nation's Deadliest Bioterror Attack*, 170.

31 Don Foster, "The Message in the Anthrax," *Vanity Fair*, as reproduced at: *http://www.ph.ucla.edu/epi/Bioter/messageanthrax.html*, October 2003.

32 The FBI first announced the Gloria Irish connection on October 14, 2001, apparently after an article appeared in *The Mail*. See, for example: Chardy, DeMarzo, and Greene, "Tabloid Editor's Wife Rented Apartment to 2 Hijackers"; Tisch, "Hijackers Linked to Tabloid"; Sean Hamill, "Editor's Wife Rented to 2 Suspects, FBI Says," *Chicago Tribune*, October 15, 2001.

33 William Broad et al, "Report Linking Anthrax and Hijackers Is Investigated," *The New York Times*, March 23, 2002.

34 Ibid.

35 Ibid.

36 Committee on Review of the Scientific Approaches Used During the FBI's Investigation of the 2001 Bacillus anthracis Mailings, *Review of the Scientific Approaches Used During the FBI's Investigation of the 2001 Anthrax Letters*, p. 66.

37 Ibid, pp. 66-67.

38 "History Commons: Complete 911 Timeline"

39 Davidsson, *Hijacking America's Mind on 9/11: Counterfeiting Evidence*, pp. 31 ff.

40 The unconvincing treatment of al-Shehhi by the 9/11 Commission il-

lustrates the point: *The 9/11 Commission Report: Final Report of the National Commission on Terrorist Attacks Upon the United States* (New York, 2004), 162.

41 A description of Mohamed Atta as someone who had "adopted fundamentalism" is quoted, apparently with approval, by the 9/11 Commission. *Ibid*, 161. But the anomalous, hedonistic behavior is described by numerous eyewitnesses. See David Griffin, *The 9/11 Commission Report: Omissions and Distortions* (Northampton, Olive Branch, 2005), p. 20. See also the material gathered at the History Commons site: http://www.historycommons.org/timeline.jsp?the_alleged_9/11_hijackers=mohamedAtta&timeline=complete_911_timeline

42 "Consensus 9/11: The 9/11 Best Evidence Panel: Point Flt-1: A Claim Regarding Hijacked Passenger Jets," n.d., http://www.consensus911.org/point-flt-1/.

43 See, for example, points PC-1, PC-1A, PC-2, PC-3, "Consensus 9/11: The Best Evidence Panel," http://www.consensus911.org/.

44 There are various accounts of the Hijackers at the Belle Glade airport. Many insist that Atta was one of the most intrusive of the visitors. Willie Lee says he went so far as to phone the police, although he does not mention Atta as the one who provoked the call: Cerabino, "Encounters with 9/11 Hijackers Still Haunt Palm Beach County Residents."

45 Ibid.

46 Ibid.

47 "History Commons: Complete 911 Timeline:" Mohamed Atta: April 26, 2001: 9/11 Hijacker Atta Given Ticket for Having No Driver's License.

48 Ibid: Mohamed Atta: December 26, 2000: 9/11 Hijackers Atta and Alshehhi Abandon Stalled Plane on Florida Runway; No Investigation Ensues.

49 Ed Vulliamy, "When Our World Changed Forever," *The Guardian*, September 16, 2001, http://www.theguardian.com/world/2001/sep/16/news.september11/print.

50 David Griffin, *Debunking 9/11 Debunking: An Answer to Popular Mechanics and Other Defenders of the Official Conspiracy Theory* (Northampton, Mass.: Olive Branch Press, 2007), 216 ff.

51 David Griffin, *The New Pearl Harbor Revisited: 9/11, the Cover-Up, and the Exposé* (Northampton, Mass.: Olive Branch, 2008), 78.

52 Jeremy Hammond, "Al Qaeda's Top Gun: Willful Deception by the 9/11 Commission," *Dissident Voice: A Radical Newsletter in the Struggle for Peace and Social Justice*, April 18, 2010, 3, http://dissidentvoice.org/2010/04/al-qaeda%E2%80%99s-top-gun-2/.

53 Ibid., 2.

54 *The 9/11 Commission Report: Final Report of the National Commission on Terrorist Attacks Upon the United States*, 530, n. 147.

55 Griffin, *Debunking 9/11 Debunking: An Answer to Popular Mechanics and Other Defenders of the Official Conspiracy Theory*, 216 ff.

56 Ibid., 218.

57 *The 9/11 Commission Report: Final Report of the National Commission*

on Terrorist Attacks Upon the United States, 225–226.

58 "Debunking the 9/11 Myths: Special Report," *Popular Mechanics*, March 2005, 217, http://www.popularmechanics.com/technology/military/news/1227842.

59 Hammond, "Al Qaeda's Top Gun: Willful Deception by the 9/11 Commission," 6.

60 Griffin, *Debunking 9/11 Debunking: An Answer to Popular Mechanics and Other Defenders of the Official Conspiracy Theory*, 217–218.

61 *The 9/11 Commission Report: Final Report of the National Commission on Terrorist Attacks Upon the United States*, 226.

62 Ibid., 226–227.

63 Hammond, "Al Qaeda's Top Gun: Willful Deception by the 9/11 Commission," 9–10.

64 Hammond even throws into question the supposed training Hanjour carried out on flight simulators that would have prepared him for flying jets. "Al Qaeda's Top Gun: Willful Deception by the 9/11 Commission," 10 ff.

65 *The 9/11 Commission Report: Final Report of the National Commission on Terrorist Attacks Upon the United States*, 531, n. 170.

66 *MEMORANDUM FOR THE RECORD: Interview of Eddie Guigui Shalev*, FBI interview of E. Shalev by Quinn John Tamm, Jr., (April 9, 2004), http://media.nara.gov/9-11/MFR/t-0148-911MFR-00551.pdf.

67 Mark Gaffney, "How the FBI and 9/11 Commission Suppressed Key Evidence about Hani Hanjour, Alleged Hijack Pilot of AAL 77," *Information Clearing House*, July 7, 2009, http://www.informationclearinghouse.info/article22999.htm.

68 Griffin, *The New Pearl Harbor Revisited: 9/11, the Cover-Up, and the Exposé*, 79. 9/11 Consensus Panel. Point Pent-3: The Claim Regarding Hani Hanjour as Flight 77 Pilot, http://www.consensus911.org/point-pent-3/

69 The story is from the *Zhan Guo Ce* (Wade-Giles, *Chan-kuo Ts'e*), "Strategems of the Warring States," composed over 2000 years ago.

70 David Griffin, *The New Pearl Harbor: Disturbing Questions about the Bush Administration and 9/11 (updated Edition)*, August, 2004 (Northampton, Mass.: Olive Branch, 2004), 87.

71 Ibid., 86.

72 Seymour Hersh, "What Went Wrong: The C.I.A. and the Failure of American Intelligence," *The New Yorker*, October 8, 2001.

73 "History Commons: Complete 911 Timeline," September 11-13: 9/11 Hijackers Leave a Clear Trail of Evidence.

74 *ANNEX TO APPENDIX TO ENCLOSURE A: PRETEXTS TO JUSTIFY US MILITARY INTERVENTION IN CUBA (OPERATION NORTHWOODS, Pp. 137 Ff.)*, 1962, 141, http://www.maryferrell.org/mffweb/archive/viewer/showDoc.do?docId=1244&relPageId=137.

75 David Griffin, *The 9/11 Commission Report: Omissions and Distortions* (Northampton, Mass.: Olive Branch Press, 2005).

76 Kelly Thornton, "Hijackers Who Lived Here: 'Nice,' 'Dull': Search of

Muslim Leader's Home May Provide More Information," *San Diego Union-Tribune*, September 16, 2001.

77 Michael Isikoff, "Exclusive: The Informant Who Lived With the Hijackers," *Newsweek*, September 16, 2002.

78 "History Commons: Complete 911 Timeline," October 5, 2002: FBI Refuses to Allow FBI Informant Who Was Landlord to Two 9/11 Hijackers to Testify before 9/11 Inquiry.

79 Ibid, September 16, 2002: Der Spiegel Claims 9/11 Hijacker Jarrah Had Spy Relative.

80 Ibid, 1983-July 2008: 9/11 Hijacker's Two Cousins Allegedly Work as Israeli Spies.

81 *Suspicious Activities Involving Israeli Art Students at DEA Facilities* (Drug Enforcement Administration (DEA), 2001), http://physics911.ca/deareport.

82 Christopher Ketcham, "The Israeli 'Art Student' Mystery ('Corrected since Its Original Publication')," *Salon*, May 7, 2002, http://www.salon.com/2002/05/07/students/.

83 Christopher Ketcham, "Cheering Movers and Art Student Spies: What Did Israel Know in Advance of the 9/11 Attacks?," *CounterPunch*, 2007, http://www.counterpunch.org/2007/03/07/what-did-israel-know-in-advance-of-the-9-11-attacks/.

84 Ibid., 4.

85 Ibid., 4,5.

86 Ibid., 5.

87 The FBI eventually claimed that there was no solid evidence of foreknowledge, but this conclusion is extremely difficult to square with evidence from eyewitnesses and from the photographs, described by the Bureau, taken by the young Israeli men. FBI documents corroborate the original FBI bulletin's claim on 9/11 that "Three individuals with van were seen celebrating after initial impact." See Ketcham, "Cheering Movers and Art Student Spies: What Did Israel Know in Advance of the 9/11 Attacks?"; Christopher Isham et al., "Were Israelis Detained on Sept. 11 Spies?," *ABC News*, June 21, 2002, http://abcnews.go.com/2020/story?id=123885&page=1&singlePage=true; "FBI Documents Relating to the So-called 'Dancing Israelis,'" n.d., http://www.scribd.com/doc/62394765/Related-article-at-http-tinyurl-com-FBI-Dancing-Israelis-Dancing-Israelis-FBI-document-Section-6-1138796-001-303A-NK-105536-Section-6.

88 "History Commons: Summer 2001: Israel Warns US of 'Big Attack'; August 8-15, 2001: Israel Reportedly Warns of Major Assault on the US; August 23, 2001: Mossad Reportedly Gives CIA List of Terrorists Living in US; at Least Four 9/11 Hijackers Named," n.d., http://www.historycommons.org/context.jsp?item=asummer01bigattack#asummer01bigattack.

89 Griffin, *The New Pearl Harbor Revisited: 9/11, the Cover-Up, and the Exposé*, 160.

90 Ibid.; "Consensus 9/11: The 9/11 Best Evidence Panel: Mohamed Atta's

Mysterious Trip to Portland: Point H-1," n.d., http://www.consensus911.org/point-h-1/.

91 Paul Duggan, "FBI Chief Promises to Give State And Local Police a Role in Probe," *The Washington Post*, October 17, 2001.

92 Ibid.

93 Massimo Calabresi and Sally Donnelly, "Cropduster Manual Discovered," *TIME*, September 22, 2001, http://www.time.com/time/nation/article/0,8599,175951,00.html.

94 Nakashima and Weiss, "Biological Attack Concerns Spur Warnings: Restoration of Broken Public Health System Is Best Preparation, Experts Say."

95 Blum and Eggen, "Crop-Dusters Thought To Interest Suspects."

96 Ibid.

97 Ibid.

98 Amanda Riddle, "Crop-Dusters a No-Go amid Fears," *Daily Iowan*, September 25, 2001.

99 Blum and Eggen, "Crop-Dusters Thought To Interest Suspects."

100 Dana Canedy, "Crop-Dusters Are Grounded on Fears of Toxic Attacks," *The New York Times*, September 25, 2001.

101 Cerabino, "Encounters with 9/11 Hijackers Still Haunt Palm Beach County Residents."

102 Canedy, "Crop-Dusters Are Grounded on Fears of Toxic Attacks."

103 Blum and Weiss, "Suspect May Have Wanted to Buy Plane; Inquiries Reported On Crop-Duster Loan."

104 Mohammad N. Akhter, "Bioterrorism: How Unready We Are," *The Washington Post*, October 10, 2001.

105 "'This Is a Time of Testing,'" *The Washington Post*, October 12, 2001.

106 Marilyn Thompson says she spoke to James Lester by phone and confirmed his story about Atta visiting the crop-dusting operation. Marilyn Thompson, *The Killer Strain: Anthrax and a Government Exposed* (New York: HarperCollins, 2003), p. 54.

107 Miller, Engelberg, and Broad, *Germs: Biological Weapons and America's Secret War*.

108 Ibid, pp. 102, 110.

109 The Monterey Institute of International Studies, (www.miis.edu) of Middlebury College prepared documentation for the Nuclear Threat Initiative (www.nti.org) called "Iraq Biological Chronology," last updated in October, 2008. For crucial years this documentation details Iraq's alleged development of biological weapons.

110 "Could Iraq Spread Death via Remote Crop Dusters?" *Deseret News*, November 9, 1997. The *Deseret News* article presents itself as dependent on an article from *The Sunday Times*.

111 Blum and Weiss, "Suspect May Have Wanted to Buy Plane; Inquiries Reported On Crop-Duster Loan."

112 "Face to Face With a Terrorist - Worker Recalls Atta Seeking Funds Before 9/11," *ABCNEWS.com*, June 6, 2002. See Elias Davidsson's insightful analysis of the incident: http://www.aldeilis.net/english/index.

php?option=com_content&view=article&id=3190:johnelle-bryants-extraordinary-meeting-with-mohamed-atta&catid=194&Itemid=333

113 Martin Bright et al, "The Secret War, Part 1: War on Terrorism," *The Observer*, September 30, 2001, http://www.guardian.co.uk/world/2001/sep/30/terrorism.afghanistan7.

114 Blum and Weiss, "Suspect May Have Wanted to Buy Plane; Inquiries Reported On Crop-Duster Loan."

115 "ABC News' Wrongest Reporter Strikes Again," *Gawker*, December 30, 2009, http://gawker.com/5437245/abc-news-wrongest-reporter-strikes-again.

116 Ibid. See also "How ABC News' Brian Ross Cooked His 'Hasan Contacted Al Qaeda' Scoop," *Gawker*, November 10, 2009, http://gawker.com/5401562/how-abc-news-brian-ross-cooked-his-hasan-contacted-al-qaeda-scoop.

117 Edward Jay Epstein, "Fictoid #11: The Terror Crop Dusters," *The Big Picture*, n.d., http://www.edwardjayepstein.com/nether_fictoid11.htm. I have based my understanding of "fictoid" on the entry in *Urban Dictionary:* http://www.urbandictionary.com/define.php?term=fictoid.

118 Sarasin, *Anthrax: Bioterror as Fact and Fantasy*, p. 156.

119 Michael Osterholm and John Schwartz, *Living Terrors: What America Needs to Know to Survive the Coming Bioterrorist Catastrophe* (New York: Dell Publishing, 2000). For the "Ed" narrative, see pp. 24 ff.

120 A hijack exercise was performed on April 19, 2000 involving a "crop duster chemical incident" in which a "Crop Duster flies over Holloman and release [sic] an areosol [sic]". Presumably "Holloman" refers to Holloman Air Force Base in New Mexico. See the NORAD Exercises Hijack Summary from the 9/11 Commission: http://www.scribd.com/doc/16411947/NORAD-Exercises-Hijack-Summary\

121 The crop duster gets a mention in Moussaoui's first indictment: *UNITED STATES OF AMERICA -v- ZACARIAS MOUSSAOUI* (United States District Court for the Eastern District of Virginia, Alexandria Division, December 2001), http://cryptome.org/usa-v-zm-ind.htm. But in the July 25, 2002 indictment the relevant section is dropped: "The old paragraph 17 in the Overt Acts has also been entirely deleted. That paragraph provided discussion of Mr. Atta making inquiries about crop dusting. That is no longer in the superseding indictment." *Ibid.*

122 "The Iraqi regime has also developed ways to disperse lethal biological agents, widely and indiscriminately into the water supply, into the air. For example, Iraq had a programme to modify aerial fuel tanks for Mirage jets. This video of an Iraqi test flight obtained by Unscom some years ago shows an Iraqi F-1 Mirage jet aircraft. Note the spray coming from beneath the Mirage; that is 2,000 liters of simulated anthrax that a jet is spraying." "Full Text of Colin Powell's Speech," *The Guardian*, February 5, 2003, http://www.theguardian.com/world/2003/feb/05/iraq.usa

123 Charles Duelfer, *Comprehensive Report of the Special Advisor to the DCI on Iraq's WMD*, September 2004; Scott Ritter, *Iraq Confidential:*

The Untold Story of the Intelligence Conspiracy to Undermine the UN and Overthrow Saddam Hussein (New York: Nation Books, 2005). The section of the 1999 report to the UNSC by the UN weapons inspectors dealing with biological weapons is also of interest, although we can see in retrospect that it was extremely unfair to Iraq: *UNSCOM - Report to the Security Council - 25 January 1999*, 1999, http://www.fas.org/news/un/iraq/s/990125/dis-bio.htm.

CHAPTER 8

THE UNTHINKABLE

In 2010 Gerald Mandell, a specialist in infectious diseases, gave a presidential address to the American Clinical and Climatological Association. The talk was entitled, "Thinking about the Unthinkable."[1] By "the unthinkable" Mandell meant a bioweapon attack on the United States. Referring to the conclusion of a U.S. commission that "a serious bioterrorism event in the US by 2013" was likely,[2] Mandell seemed to have no doubts about who would be the perpetrator. The chief danger was from "evil elements in Islam." "These people," he said, "want to kill all who don't follow their fanatical religiosity." Unlike previous enemies of the U.S., Mandell said, these evil elements in Islam are not rational and thus constitute "a truly diabolical threat." In addition to the fact that "they have no qualms about killing children, women, and other non-combatants," they have no fear of death. Indeed, "many of them actually wish to die, as is evidenced by suicide bombers and pilots of planes used as missiles."

Mandell, writing in 2010, was not the first to speak of a bioweapons attack as "the unthinkable" or to refer to thinking about the unthinkable.

An editorial in *The New York Times* on October 7, 2001, two days after Robert Stevens' death, announced that, "[p]anicky citizens have been trying to obtain and hoard Cipro or other drugs to use if the unthinkable happens."[3]

On October 10, Mohammad Akhter, executive director of the American Public Health Association and former commissioner of public health for the District of Columbia, in an article in the *Washington Post* entitled, "Bioterrorism: How Unready We Are," wrote: "Along with nuclear war, a pandemic sparked by an act of terrorism that kills hundreds of thousands of people is the ultimate health crisis. As difficult as it is to think about such a nightmare scenario, we must begin preparing now for the unthinkable."[4]

On October 14, the *Sunday Mercury*, a tabloid from Birmingham in the U.K., entitled an article: "Anthrax: Why We Must Now Think the Unthinkable."[5] In this article we learn that "Chief Medical Officer Dr. Liam Donaldson, who has just returned from a trip to the US, said: 'The ground rules are still the same, but I think we have to now be prepared over the future to think the unthinkable.'"

An article in *USA Today* on October 15, 2001, referring to bioweapons (smallpox) attacks, suggested that the possibility "was only a few weeks ago unthinkable."[6]

The day after the *USA Today* article appeared (Oct. 16), the *St. Petersburg Times* began an article: "The unfolding unthinkable of an anthrax outbreak..."[7]

The following day (Oct. 17) CNN reported that, according to U.S. Health and Human Services Secretary Tommy Thompson, "we are taking all the steps necessary to keep America safe in an era when biological and chemical attacks are as possible as they are unthinkable.'"[8]

On October 23 *The New York Times* had a long multiple-author article with the title, "On Many Fronts, Experts Plan for the Unthinkable: Biowarfare."[9] Here we learn that Dr. Frank Bia, "an expert on infectious diseases and microbiology at Yale," believes that "the unthinkable has become thinkable."

There is a pattern here. The pattern may not signify a

grand plan, or, indeed, conscious intent at all—there may be no conspiracy—but, whatever the origins of the "unthinkable" discourse, it deserves investigation and contemplation.

For many years before 2001 "the unthinkable" had been used, among those who studied and participated in American war strategy, to refer to nuclear war. This usage is generally traced to Herman Kahn, who initiated it in his famous 1960 book, *On Thermonuclear War*, and reinforced it in a second book, *Thinking about the Unthinkable* (1962).[10] Kahn's writings gave the term a quasi-technical status, which was accepted by many subsequent writers.

The expression was adopted even by many of those who were strongly critical of the nuclear strategizing of Kahn and others. For example, when Brian Easlea decided in the early 1980s to write a book about the connections between patriarchy and nuclear weapons he entitled it: *Fathering the Unthinkable: Masculinity, Scientists and the Nuclear Arms Race*.[11]

Many of the references in the October news reports quoted above dealing with bioweapons, especially those that refer to thinking the unthinkable, have clearly been influenced by this decades-old tradition in strategic thinking.

Why does this matter? It matters because "the unthinkable" is an expression that functioned to help launch a new conflict framework, the Global War on Terror. There are two instances of the use of "the unthinkable" in 2001 that are especially useful in clarifying this.

The First Unthinkable

We may begin by considering the period from May 1 to December 13, 2001.

In 1972 the United States and the Soviet Union had signed the Antiballistic Missile Treaty.[12] The treaty became one of the pillars of the Cold War strategy of nuclear deterrence. In signing the treaty the superpowers undertook to renounce the attempt to build weapons of defense against nuclear missiles. They agreed, in effect, to leave themselves vulnerable: each would forego military defense on the understanding that the prospect of nuclear retaliation by the enemy was so horrifying that each side would be *deterred* from attacking the other. This was an unusual agreement in the history of warfare and it arose due to the spectacular destructiveness of nuclear weapons as well as the fact that no technology had been invented that could offer a significant defense against intercontinental ballistic missiles.

On May 1, 2001, George W. Bush, in a major foreign policy speech, gave informal public notice that the United States intended to withdraw unilaterally from the ABM Treaty.[13] The Treaty allowed a signatory to withdraw as long as that signatory gave six months notice and was able to cite "extraordinary events" that have "jeopardized its supreme interests."[14] Though no such events had taken place at the time of his May 1 speech, the events of the fall of 2001 would allow Bush to give formal notice of intention to withdraw from the treaty on December 13.

Bush's May 1 speech was delivered at the National Defense University at Fort McNair in Washington, D.C.[15] Attending were those who would be expected to attend an announcement of such strategic significance: Secretary of Defense Donald Rumsfeld, Secretary of State Colin Powell, National Security Council Advisor Condoleezza Rice, Vice Chairman of the Joint Chiefs of Staff General Richard Myers, and various military officers of high rank. In giving notice that this major treaty would be abandoned, Bush deployed the rhetoric we would expect, the quasi-mythical rhetoric of the good nation (the U.S.) versus the bad nation (the Soviet Union), of freedom versus tyranny, and so on. He announced that the withdrawal from the treaty was, in most respects, a sign of human progress. The evil Soviet Union existed no more and its successor, Russia, was democratic and was not an enemy of the United States. Therefore, cuts in nuclear arsenals were possible, Cold War thinking could be cast aside, and the possibility of peace could best be seized by leaving behind relics of a previous era such as the ABM Treaty.

Along with his celebration of the end of the Cold War, Bush inserted warnings of new dangers. While nuclear weapons possessed by the superpowers were less dangerous than in previous times, "weapons of mass destruction," a category that at the time referred mainly to nuclear, chemical and biological weapons, constituted a growing threat in so far as both the weapons and the technology to deliver them by missiles were becoming widely disseminated. Increasingly, weapons of mass destruction (also called "weapons of terror" in this speech) would be available to "some of the world's least responsible states." U.S. policy, Bush said, had to change to accommodate these developments. Strategy must now focus on meeting these new threats and finding ways to defend the U.S. from such irresponsible states.

When he spoke of making the shift to what he called a "new framework," Bush said the U.S. *must be willing to "rethink the unthinkable."* Although he was not the first person to speak of rethinking the unthinkable, the expression had not been used on a comparably important occasion.[16] What was indicated here was a conscious shifting of the chief danger to the United States. No longer were the Soviet Union and its massive nuclear arsenal the chief dangers. In their stead stood an assortment of countries, many small and poor, with a rag-tag collection of weapons of widely varying destructiveness. To rethink the unthinkable in this context meant to be aware of new unimaginable horrors: (i) terrorism and (ii) rogue states with "weapons of mass destruction." These two horrors would be given credibility a few months later as actual lethal operations in the U.S. homeland. The 9/11 attacks were acts of terrorism, while, if the Double Perpetrator hypothesis were to be accepted, the anthrax attacks represented an attack by a rogue state using a weapon of mass destruction.

The May 1 speech was, as mentioned, couched in quasi-mythical language. The actual aim of the new orientation had already been expressed in more straightforward terms in the year 2000 in the famous document, *Rebuilding America's Defenses* (RAD), a production of the neoconservative Project for the New American Century (PNAC).[17] There was a great overlap between those participating in PNAC and those who had spent their time trying to find a way to invade and take over Iraq after the failure of the George H. W. Bush administration to do so in 1991.

Rebuilding America's Defenses was an endorsement of a frankly imperial American destiny. The neoconservative authors of the document had no interest in a global order in which the United States would take its place as a state among states, bound by international law and accountable to international institutions.

A simple word study gives an indication of where the authors of RAD situated themselves.

- "United Nations" and "UN" occur altogether four times in the document: each mention is brief and three of the four references are negative and dismissive.

- Although the term "security" occurs 94 times, the term "Security Council" does not occur.

- The expression "international law" does not occur.

- The terms "treaty" and "treaties" occur altogether 9 times, referring to non-proliferation treaties, the Comprehensive Test Ban Treaty, and the Anti-ballistic Missile Treaty: every reference is negative, stressing the inconvenience of treaties for *Pax Americana.*

Essentially, in RAD the possibility of using, strengthening or developing institutions of global cooperation, whether related to policing, law, culture or anything else, is put aside. The importance of friends and allies is acknowledged, but it is assumed that the U.S. will exert dominance in such relationships.

Given the close connections between PNAC and the George W. Bush administration, it is no surprise that, as Senator Tom Daschle notes in his memoirs, within months of taking office, Bush:

> walked away from agreements that had been embraced by many of our closest friends and allies and broadly supported by the international community: The Comprehensive Test Ban Treaty, efforts to create an international criminal court, the Biological Weapons Protocol, the Kyoto Protocol, and the Anti-Ballistic Missile Treaty.

One of the key recommendations of RAD had to do with the last of these, the ABM Treaty. The document recommends: "Develop and deploy global missile defenses to defend the American homeland and American allies, and to provide a secure basis for U.S. power projection around the world."[18] In other words: a functional and effective defense capability is needed to enable a policy of aggression or the threat of same, by overcoming the barrier of fear of retaliation. The need for such missile defenses is one of the main themes of RAD. The 1972 ABM Treaty was explicitly targeted in this document as an obstacle to the achievement of this goal.[19] (Note that while the nuclear arms race provided the original context of the ABM Treaty, the text of the Treaty does not speak of nuclear weapons but of "strategic ballistic missiles," which can be interpreted to include non-nuclear ballistic missiles with any sort of WMD aimed at the U.S. homeland.)

RAD's authors wanted to see a new framework for

American power: they wanted to move beyond Cold War constraints to an era of expanded U.S. global dominance. This could not be achieved while small states were free to brandish their third world variants on weapons of mass destruction.

A careful reading of RAD reveals that its authors were not worried that some country with a tiny arsenal of biological or chemical weapons (or nuclear weapons, for that matter) was going to decide to initiate a suicidal strike on the U.S. homeland. The concern, rather, was that the possession of these weapons might give to such countries the clout to successfully deter the U.S.—either through a threat against the U.S. homeland or a threat against U.S. allies or "expeditionary forces abroad."[20] In one of its most strikingly honest statements RAD says: "In the post-Cold War era, America and its allies, rather than the Soviet Union, have become the primary objects of deterrence and it is states like Iraq, Iran and North Korea who most want to develop deterrent capabilities."[21] Obviously, the desire for "deterrent capabilities" came from worries that the U.S. and its allies might have aims inimical to the security or interests of these countries.

The development of missile defense by the U.S. has, in RAD, little to do with "defense" in the sense that most U.S. citizens would understand the term. It has to do with permitting U.S. forces to achieve military dominance—to go where they wish and do what they want without worrying about regional powers that oppose their intervention. Once the ABM Treaty was disposed of, the U.S. could, without inhibitions, develop the technology that would allow all missile threats from small states to be dealt with, thereby leaving those states at the mercy of U.S. forces.

The worry of U.S. neoconservatives in 2001 was, apparently, that the U.S. public would not accept repudiation of treaties, costly new military programs, and the shift to a new global conflict framework—from Cold War to Global War on Terror—unless this public was convinced the changes were necessary for achieving legitimate goals. And presumably these neoconservatives were worried that U.S. dominance of the globe might not be perceived as such.

The May 1 informal withdrawal announcement and the December 13 formal announcement of withdrawal from the ABM treaty were the result of a top-down decision made by a small number of men engaging in minimal consultation with others inside the U.S. security community.[22] Likewise, although there was rhetoric about consulting allies, including former adversary Russia, this process was rushed and was not permitted to change the decision that had been made. Putin, for example, never agreed with the decision to terminate the ABM treaty. He simply had no choice but to live with it and to extract small concessions in other areas.

Not surprisingly, after the 9/11 attacks Bush used 9/11 to further justify repudiation of the ABM treaty—a treaty he now spoke of openly as antiquated and dangerous.[23] As the violent events of the fall unfolded, opponents of his decision to withdraw from the ABM Treaty within the Democratic Party fell silent.[24]

Although Putin expressed sympathy for the U.S. after the 9/11 events, he did not acknowledge Bush's logic.[25] Why should non-state terrorists, such as were supposed to have carried out the 9/11 attacks, be treated as if they were states? What, to put it bluntly, did such terrorist groups have to do with discussions and treaties clearly framed for states? Where were the missiles? Where were the nuclear weapons or other weapons of mass destruction? But Putin was not heeded. Although Powell apparently wished to slow down the pace and offer Putin more concessions, he was pushed aside by those, including Bush, Cheney and Rumsfeld, who had decided to proceed quickly without Russian approval.

The December 13 speech by Bush was, compared to that of May 1, perfunctory, but if we examine it carefully we will notice a significant problem.[26] Although 9/11 occupies a position of importance, the omission of all reference to the anthrax attacks creates a telling space. Recall that Bush, in pulling the U.S. out of this very important treaty, was obligated to provide a statement of the "extraordinary events" that justified withdrawal. In his speech 9/11 had to serve as the extraordinary event, but it did not accomplish the job. The 9/11 attacks, however horrific, seemed to have little to do with the ABM Treaty, even if the treaty were interpreted broadly. There was no ballistic missile, no nuclear weapons, not even a "weapon of mass destruction" as that expression was customarily used at the time. Putin had already pointed out the difficulty.

Here are two sentences that represent the best Bush was able to do in his December 13 address:

> 1. "I have concluded the ABM Treaty hinders our government's ability to develop ways to protect our people from future terrorist or rogue-state attacks."
>
> 2. "Today, as the events of September the 11th made all too clear, the greatest threats to both our countries come not from each other, or other big powers in the world, but from terrorists who strike without warning, or rogue states who seek weapons of mass destruction."

Statement 2 is incoherent. What did the events of September the 11th have to do with rogue states seeking weapons of mass destruction? By December 13 the White House had already dropped the claim that al-Qaeda and/or Iraq were responsible for the anthrax attacks. Since it was now clear that the anthrax attacks were a domestic operation, these attacks could not be drawn on to support Bush's ABM argument and, in fact, had to be studiously ignored. But if the story of the Double Perpetrator, pushed so hard in October and apparently planned from the outset, had succeeded, Bush could have cogently said: "Today, as the events of September the 11th and the subsequent anthrax attacks made all too clear, the greatest threats...come...from terrorists who strike without warning, and their rogue state sponsors who possess weapons of mass destruction." Bush would simply have had to add that such rogue states with WMD also had long-range missiles to deliver their WMD. His administration was, in fact, fraudulently claiming this very thing about Iraq at the time. These are the kinds of statement Bush could have been expected to make if the Double Perpetrator frame-up had worked. When it failed it left him exposed. He had no convincing "extraordinary event" such as was required for withdrawal from the Treaty.

The expression, "the unthinkable," whether part of a plan or not, functioned as part of a transitional discourse, taking citizens from the horrors of the Cold War to the horrors of the new conflict framework, the Global War on Terror. In each case the horrors were supposed to be beyond the imaginative capacity of citizens.

A second curious instance of "the unthinkable" adds weight to the idea that a plan was involved.

The Second Unthinkable

On October 12, 2001 the news media announced that Erin O'Connor, an assistant to Tom Brokaw at NBC news, had tested positive for cutaneous anthrax. Employees at NBC remembered that a letter had been received at NBC, postmarked in St. Petersburg, Florida on September 20 and addressed to Tom Brokaw.[27] The letter had contained a threat and a quantity of white powder. The enclosed message had announced itself with the words: "the unthinkable."[28]

In early analyses of the anthrax attacks, this letter played a prominent role. Even when it was discovered that the white powder was harmless and that a letter from New Jersey, postmarked on September 18, had contained the anthrax spores that infected O'Connor, it was assumed by many that the September 20 letter was part of the operation.[29]

The September 20 threat letter was apparently one of a set of three from St. Petersburg, the others arriving at their destinations in October. One went to Howard Troxler at the *St. Petersburg Times* and one to Judith Miller at her *New York Times* office. The conclusion that the three were a set was based not only on identical locations of origin and similar dates of postage, but on quite specific peculiarities in the writing.[30]

It would take us too far afield to discuss these threat letters in detail and, in any case, the September 20 letter has not been released to the public. But Don Foster, an English professor who was given access by the FBI to the September 20 letter, says the following about the text:

> The letter, postmarked on September 20 in St. Petersburg, Florida, began:
>
> "THE UNTHINKABEL"
> SAMPLE OF HOW IT WILL LOOK[31]

The letter went on to threaten bioterror attacks on various targets. The capital Ns in "THE UNTHINKABEL" were printed backwards, and Foster comments that they "resembled the letter I in Russia's Cyrillic alphabet." Foster does not pretend to know why "the unthinkable" was put in quotation marks and spelled wrong, although he comments that it "looked like a deliberate misspelling" and adds that the quotation marks "were done Russian-style." He says it was possible that through the use of these quotation marks and through the backward Ns someone was attempting "to make his writing look Russian."

Foster caught a number of interesting features of this document but he also passed over important clues. He noted that a related letter was sent to Judith Miller, but he ought to have mentioned that Russia gets pride of place in her October, 2001 book as the most dangerous source of bioweapons. Iraq comes second and is dangerous, in part, because it was supposedly receiving biological material from the Russians. During this entire period Miller, a participant in Dark Winter and a known deceiver about Iraq's WMD, was continuing, through her book and her work for *The New York Times,* to promote the threat from the Russia-Iraq axis.

As for the term "the unthinkable," Foster did not mention the history of the term (Kahn) or Bush's May 1 employment of it. He also did not seem to be aware of how commonly the term was mobilized in October of 2001 to announce the anthrax attacks and to indicate that the United States was entering a new era in which a "new framework" would be required.

The relationship of "the unthinkable" in the September 20 letter to the various October speeches and media articles is problematic. The letter cannot be copying the articles in the papers and speeches because it was sent before the proliferation of the term in October. And, on the other hand, the great majority of the articles in the media and speeches cannot be inspired by this letter because, although it was sent on September 20th, its text was apparently not revealed to the public until October 22, after many of these articles and speeches were written.[32]

So sits the St. Petersburg UNTHINKABEL, awkward and unexplained.

Although it may seem obvious that the St. Petersburg letter postmarked on September 20 was part of the anthrax attacks, some investigators, including the FBI,[33] have denied this. But the evidence suggests the September 20 letter was part of the operation. (See Appendix for reasons why the denials are unconvincing.) There is, in this case, no mystery as to why it had to be swept into oblivion. Why would al-Qaeda or Iraq have referred to a biological attack as "the unthinkable?" Misspelling the word and using backward Ns does not help. Implying a Russian connection in this way is equally implausible. The truth is that the employment of "the unthinkable" in this letter, when weight is given both to the meaning of the term in U.S. strategic circles and to the other relevant uses of the term in 2001, points us in the direction of the U.S. military and intelligence communities.

But why would anyone include such an obvious road sign in the first place? We can only speculate. Perhaps those who penned the letter did not see it as an obvious road sign. Perhaps they were right: it appears that "the unthinkable" in this letter has largely avoided scrutiny.

Is the September 20 threat letter compatible with the FBI's Bruce Ivins hypothesis? It is not. Consider the difficulty of the location from which this letter, and its two companion letters, was sent. The FBI was not even able to show that Ivins had driven secretly from his home in Frederick, Maryland to Princeton, New Jersey to mail the anthrax letters that had been sent from that location. The best the Bureau was able to do was to argue that he *could have made it to Princeton and back*.[34] How much more difficult it would be to argue that he sneaked away repeatedly to St. Petersburg, Florida during this period! (If he went by car a return trip to Princeton, New Jersey would have taken about 6.5 hours, whereas each return trip to St. Petersburg would have consumed about 30 hours.) At the very least he would have needed an accomplice, and this would signal the end of the lone wolf hypothesis. This was explained by Barbara Rosenberg years ago.[35] It has been pushed aside because it is an embarrassment to the FBI's hypothesis.

The Meaning and Implications of the Unthinkable

For Herman Kahn, however natural the recoiling of the mind before horrific weapons, this shrinking away from reality must be resisted with "an act of iron will."[36] One *must* think about the unthinkable. The neoconservatives who have exerted so much influence in U.S. politics in recent decades appear to have taken Kahn's admonition to heart for themselves, but there is no sign they have ever wished ordinary citizens to do likewise. Citizens are meant to be afraid, to be anxious—likewise, Congress—and to hand over power to the executive branch, which will protect and save them.

Citizens are exposed to horrors, are victims of horrors, and are told to believe that a new evil that passes all bounds has them in its sights. To use Gerald Mandell's words, the new danger is "evil elements in Islam." Although the evil elements in Islam may not possess the firepower of the old enemy, the Soviet Union, the Soviets were rational whereas the new enemy is not. Moreover, although the Soviet Union threatened the U.S. homeland with destruction, it never actually followed through on the threat. Evil elements in Islam, on the other hand, have successfully targeted the homeland to devastating effect.

Citizens need not imagine biowarfare in detail; they need not ponder "the unthinkable." The executive branch will take care of all that.

While we need not ascribe special profundity to the neoconservative usage of "the unthinkable," it is clear that one of the tasks of the term within the ideological vocabulary of this group has been to mark off the conceptually forbidden, and to thereby serve particular ways of thinking and the elites associated with such thinking.

And how will the executive, thus given power by the childlike citizenry and the cowed legislative branch, deal with the new threat? How will it respond to terrorist groups and rogue states led by evil elements in Islam? Why, in any way it sees fit, and with whatever force it believes appropriate.

In Chapter 5 Jeff Stein's comment was noted: "few Americans, in their present angry and anxious mood, can imagine weeping much if Baghdad is nuked while millions here are dying from smallpox." Although this might have seemed too fantastical a scenario for the public to take seriously, perhaps it was not.

On October 19, 2001, in the midst of the anthrax attacks, Dick Cheney, standing in front of "a huge backdrop of the American flag and a dais full of New York's top political figures," told a white-tie gathering at the Waldorf-Astoria: "We must and we will use every means at our disposal to ensure the security and freedom of the American people."[37]

Journalist Dana Milbank commented:

> Some in the Bush administration have supported a more explicit threat to use American nuclear weapons to deter or combat massive biological or chemical attacks on the United States, and though he used no specific language last night, Cheney said that "no punishment for the terrorist seems too harsh." Promising a fight that will last generations and sometimes employ unsavory tactics, he added: "The struggle can only end with their complete and permanent destruction."[38]

There was much that was worrisome in Milbank's article, as well as in Cheney's speech, and it appears from Gerald Mandell's address that between 2001 and 2010 not much had changed. Mandell pushed hard in his 2010 address to put the bioweapons of the "evil elements in Islam" on the same level as the nuclear weapons of the U.S. Ever since the first Gulf War of 1991 the "weapons of mass destruction" discourse has been used to accomplish this. If the chemical or biological weapons of a small state, however pathetic their destructive potential, can be listed as WMD and conveniently put in the same category as the U.S. nuclear arsenal, half the battle has already been won. The U.S. population can in this case be made to regard the country in question as an existential threat comparable to the former Soviet Union and can be induced to regard invasion and occupation as necessary "defense."

In Mandell's speech, the attempt to equate these different arsenals reached its peak with a criticism of President Obama for stating that he would not necessarily order the use of nuclear weapons as a response to a bioweapon attack on the U.S. Mandell wanted this changed. If "these people" attack the U.S. homeland with bioweapons, the U.S. president should be ready to reply with the U.S. nuclear arsenal.

Imagine what this bellicose position might lead to in the real world. Picture an attack in the U.S. similar to the anthrax attacks of 2001 but with more casualties. Now imagine well groomed television anchors interviewing "experts" who solemnly tell their audience that, via a Muslim "terrorist group," the bioweapon has come from Syria or Iran. U.S. leaders, with every show of reluctance but with the determination of outraged patriotism, wheel out small nuclear weapons ("mini-nukes") for strikes on the state in question. The U.S. population is assured the strikes are carefully targeted at production facilities. The aim, explains the President, is simply to destroy evil technology so that the rogue state will no longer be able to threaten the U.S. with its weapons of mass destruction.

In addition to the devastation visited on Syria or Iran, the "nuclear firebreak"—that crucial division between nuclear weapons and all other sorts of weapons—would in this case be nullified. No one knows where this might lead.

When Mandell gave his address he was a member of the Medical Advisory Board of GIDEON, the Global Infectious Disease and Epidemiology Network.[39] Whatever the merits of this organization, its founder and CEO is a former Commander in the Israel Defense Forces Intelligence Corps.[40] Given how closely Mandell's words on the dangers of extremist Islam resemble familiar Israeli government discourse, we have a right to be profoundly suspicious of the aims of his speech.

Meanwhile, whatever we think of Mandell's nuclear advocacy, there is a genuine "unthinkable" hiding in the shadows that is quite different from the one he wishes us to contemplate. What is unthinkable for many, including, it appears, members of the U.S. legislative branch, is that in the fall of 2001 elements in the executive branch of the U.S. government collaborated in the killing of innocent citizens in the U.S. and in the attempt to kill Senators. In this way, they furthered their own aims, which included curtailing the freedoms of the U.S. population and carrying out the supreme international crime of aggression against other nations.

Endnotes

1 Gerald Mandell, "President's Address: Thinking about the Unthinkable," *Transactions of the American Clinical and Climatological Association* 122 (2011): 1–10.

2 Bob Graham and Jim Talent, *World at Risk: The Report of the Commission on the Prevention of Weapons of Mass Destruction Proliferation and Terrorism*, Report from the US Senate and House of Representatives, (2008, 2010 2007).

3 "Editorial: Fears of Anthrax and Smallpox," *The New York Times*, October 7, 2001.

4 Akhter, "Bioterrorism: How Unready We Are."

5 Emma Pinch, "Anthrax: Why We Must Now Think the Unthinkable," *Sunday Mercury*, October 14, 2001.

6 Laura Parker, Traci Watson, and Kevin Johnson, "Anthrax Incidents Create Growing Sense of Anxiety," *USA TODAY*, October 15, 2001.

7 "ABC Producer's Son Tests Positive For Anthrax," *St. Petersburg Times*, October 16, 2001, http://www.sptimes.com/News/101601/news_pf/Worldandnation/ABC_producer_s_son_te.shtml.

8 New Anthrax Exposure Cases in Senate," *CNN*, October 17, 2001, http://articles.cnn.com/2001-10-17/health/anthrax_1_anthrax-spores-hart-senate-office-building-anthrax-exposure?_s=PM:HEALTH.

9 "On Many Fronts, Experts Plan for the Unthinkable: Biowarfare," *The New York Times*, October 23, 2001.

10 Herman Kahn, *On Thermonuclear War* (Princeton: Princeton Univ. Press, 1960); Herman Kahn, *Thinking about the Unthinkable* (New York: Avon Books, 1962).

11 Brian Easlea, *Fathering the Unthinkable: Masculinity, Scientists and the Nuclear Arms Race* (London: Pluto Press, 1983).

12 "Treaty Between the United States of America and the Union of Soviet Socialist Republics on the Limitation of Anti-Ballistic Missile Systems," May 26, 1972, http://www.state.gov/t/isn/trty/16332.htm.

13 George W. Bush, "Remarks at the National Defense University (Public Papers of the Presidents of the United States: GEORGE W. BUSH)" (U.S. Government Printing Office, 2001), http://www.gpo.gov/fdsys/pkg/

PPP-2001-book1/html/PPP-2001-book1-doc-pg470-3.htm.

14 From Article XV: "Each Party shall, in exercising its national sovereignty, have the right to withdraw from this Treaty if it decides that extraordinary events related to the subject matter of this Treaty have jeopardized its supreme interests. It shall give notice of its decision to the other Party six months prior to withdrawal from the Treaty. Such notice shall include a statement of the extraordinary events the notifying Party regards as having jeopardized its supreme interests." "Treaty Between the United States of America and the Union of Soviet Socialist Republics on the Limitation of Anti-Ballistic Missile Systems."

15 Bush names the dignitaries attending his speech at the beginning of his address. Bush, "Remarks at the National Defense University (Public Papers of the Presidents of the United States: GEORGE W. BUSH)."

16 An example of an early use of the expression is: Leon Sigal, "Rethinking the Unthinkable," *Foreign Policy* No. 34 (1979): 35–51.

17 Thomas Donnelly, Donald Kagan, and Gary Schmitt, *Rebuilding America's Defenses: Strategy, Forces and Resources For a New Century* (The Project for the New American Century, September 2000).

18 Ibid, pp. iv-v.

19 "The administration's devotion to the 1972 Anti-Ballistic Missile (ABM) Treaty with the Soviet Union has frustrated development of useful ballistic missile defenses." Ibid, p. 52.

20 Ibid, p. 54.

21 Ibid.

22 My remarks about the withdrawal from the ABM treaty depend heavily on Lynn Rusten, *U.S. Withdrawal from the Antiballistic Missile Treaty* (Washington, D.C.: Center for the Study of Weapons of Mass Destruction, National Defense University, January 2010).

23 "'This Is a Time of Testing.'"

24 "Democrats in Senate Back Down on Missile Shield," *The New York Times*, September 22, 2001.

25 Mike Allen and Philip P. Pan, "Bush and Putin Edge Closer to Missile Deal," *The Washington Post*, October 22, 2001.

26 *U.S. Withdrawal From the ABM Treaty: President Bush's Remarks and U.S. Diplomatic Notes*, December 13, 2001, http://www.armscontrol.org/act/2002_01-02/docjanfeb02.

27 David Barstow, "Anthrax Found in NBC News Aide," *The New York Times*, October 13, 2001; Joshua Robin and Rocco Parascandola, "Letter to Brokaw Traced," *Newsday*, October 14, 2001.

28 The first purported quotations from this letter that I have found occur in an October 22 article: "Anxious About Anthrax: A Few Cases Do Not an Epidemic Make," *Newsweek*, October 22, 2001. According to this article, the letter started out: "The unthinkable. See what happens next."

29 Robin and Parascandola, "Letter to Brokaw Traced"; Foster, "The Message in the Anthrax."

30 Foster, "The Message in the Anthrax."

31 Ibid.

32 "Anxious About Anthrax: A Few Cases Do Not an Epidemic Make."

33 There is not a single reference to the September 20 St. Petersburg letter in the Department of Justice's Amerithrax report.

34 "Amerithrax Investigative Summary (Released Pursuant to the Freedom of Information Act)," pp. 86-87.

35 "A photograph of one hoax letter (to St. Petersburg Times) has been published, and descriptions or comparisons of others have been reported. If analysis confirms that the hoax letters were sent by the anthrax perpetrator, their postmarks will indicate his itinerary (or the assistance of an accomplice)..." Barbara Hatch Rosenberg. Various 2002 writings, archived here: http://www.anthraxinvestigation.com/anthraxreport.htm

36 Kahn, *On Thermonuclear War*.

37 Dana Milbank, "Terrorists Will Face Justice, Cheney Vows; Vice President Visits Ground Zero in N.Y.," *The Washington Post*, October 19, 2001.

38 Ibid.

39 http://www.gideononline.com/about/advisory/

40 GIDEON received a positive review in JAMA (Journal of the American Medical Association) in 2005: http://www.gideononline.com/reviews/jama2005/. I would recommend, however, that its work related to bio-terrorism be approached with caution. CEO Uri Blackman's credentials can be found here: http://www.gideononline.com/about/team/

CHAPTER 9

CONCLUSION

This book's Introduction set out a number of claims and promised that evidence would be offered to support each of them. Here is a quick review.

(a) The anthrax letter attacks were carried out by a *group* of perpetrators, not by a lone wolf.

As was shown, previous researchers have argued convincingly that the physical characteristics of the prepared anthrax spores used in the attacks indicate that, although the anthrax certainly came from a U.S. lab, the FBI's "anthrax killer," Bruce Ivins, could not have been responsible for the attacks. This book has carried the argument against a lone perpetrator further, tracing, with attention to timeline and motive, the construction of fictional scenarios intended to direct attention away from the true perpetrators and onto foreign groups useful as targets of the Global War on Terror. The work required for this construction would have been impossible for any individual to manage.

Could an individual establish the crop-duster incidents and narratives? Or establish the other connections between the Hijackers and the anthrax—for example, the detailed Florida connections discussed in Chapter 7? Would this individual have been able to write speeches for members of the executive branch, repeatedly warning of biological weapons in the lead-up to the attacks? Who sent journalists scrambling hither and yon to spread fear and anxiety about the ubiquitous al-Qaeda and to frame Iraq relentlessly and fraudulently? What about getting allegations and rumors of imminent biological attacks reported soberly in print media from the *Guardian* to *The New York Times*? Who decided to shut down the investigation after naming a lone wolf, Bruce Ivins, as anthrax killer based on cherry-picked, weak and circumstantial evidence? What individual could have sought to manage the transition from one global conflict framework (Cold War) to another (Global War on Terror) with maximum use of both the 9/11 and the anthrax attacks?

No loner, however well positioned, could have managed these things.

(b) The group that perpetrated this crime included deep insiders within the U.S. executive branch.

Whether the anthrax attacks were a top-secret government-approved initiative of the upper levels of the executive or initiated secretly by a sub-group of deep insiders, it would seem that the capacities brought to bear are available only to those who can implement policy goals.

While Bruce Ivins could be called a member of the military-industrial complex—he worked at the United States Army Medical Research Institute of Infectious Diseases—he had neither the required inside information nor the extensive connections and capabilities of the team of insiders to which the evidence points. The questions asked under point (a) indicate not merely a team but a very powerful team with high level inside knowledge and connections.

Naming suspects has not been my primary intention. However, certain groups and organizations, based on both ideology and personal connections, have emerged as what we might call "organizations of interest." These include now defunct and overlapping associations of neoconservatives with ties to the executive branch such as "the Wolfowitz cabal" and the Project for the New American Century. Their persistent use of deception, over many years, to link Iraq to al-Qaeda and to construct scenarios and fictions to justify the invasion and occupation of Iraq, have been well documented.[1]The material presented in this book simply makes visible another possible aspect of their activities that is even darker.

There have been years of research on the anomalies of the events of 9/11 that would have to be taken into account in any attempt to name the individual perpetrators of the anthrax attacks. Any naming of 9/11 suspects such as Kevin Ryan's in a recent book would have to be studied carefully in relation to the anthrax attacks to ascertain how the two sets of planners might be related to each other.[2] Given the connections between the two operations, overlapping management can be expected.

Institutions, corporate and state, outside the U.S. would also have to be investigated. (Here is where Quadrants 2 and 4 from Chapter 5 unite: a domestic group could have invited participation from a foreign group.) Researchers have made the case for involvement of intelligence agencies from several countries in the 9/11 events. While intelligence connections in Saudi Arabia and Pakistan, to mention but two, have been documented, Israel must also be included in the list of suspects. If this move leads to accusations of anti-Semitism the accusers must be answered assertively. Israel is a state and is to be held responsible for its actions like any other state.

How about the FBI? How does it fit into the anthrax case? The Bureau appears to have been the main organization that shut down the attempt to pin the crime on the Double Perpetrator in October of 2001. How do we explain this if the FBI was a partner in the crime?

The term "limited hangout" has been in circulation for years (it supposedly originated with a comment of

Richard Nixon)[3] to indicate "a public relations or propaganda technique that involves the release of previously hidden information in order to prevent a greater exposure of more important details."[4] Citizens can be allowed to feel they now have the crucial facts; certain parties can come forward to accept blame for minor mistakes; and, in the meantime, the truly important facts are kept deeply hidden.

By late October or early November of 2001 the FBI had resorted to a limited hangout position--the lone domestic perpetrator. This position enabled the Bureau to acknowledge a U.S. military source of the spores while drawing attention away from the true perpetrators and their aims. Even today, some skeptics argue about who was "the anthrax killer," unaware that they have accepted a category (the lone wolf), that evidence shows is untenable.

Nowadays few people seem to remember the anthrax attacks. Every time there is a new incident—the Boston Marathon bombing, for instance—the anthrax attacks seem to grow dimmer in the collective consciousness. ("They were so long ago...and didn't the FBI find the guy?") This amnesia is a sign of the success of the FBI cover-up.

(c) This group of perpetrators was linked to, or identical with, the perpetrators of the 9/11 attacks.

The FBI claims to have examined the relationship between the anthrax attacks and the Hijackers and to have found nothing worth pursuing—once the Double Perpetrator hypothesis had to be abandoned. Although there were roughly 285 million people living in the U.S. in 2001, we are to believe it was mere coincidence that two of the Hijackers had the same real estate agent as the first person to die of anthrax. The fact that investigators connected nine of the 19 Hijackers to one of the apartments this real estate agent located leaves the FBI unmoved. This is an instance where the FBI's determination to adopt a limited hangout position is clear. If the Bureau had been genuinely interested in solving the crime it would have relentlessly investigated the anthrax-Hijackers scenarios, seeking the group that had constructed these scenarios to frame al-Qaeda.

Chapter 7 showed that the detailed Florida connections cannot be dismissed. Nor can the other dozen or so events or stories that at one time (before the spores were shown to have a domestic source) were held to link the perpetrators of the 9/11 and of the anthrax attacks. The perpetrators—the deep insiders responsible for the anthrax attacks—initially worked hard to make a Hijacker-anthrax connection appear convincing. Putting the date "09-11-01" in the notes accompanying the deadly spores was only the most obvious of their moves. When the FBI began leading people off in the direction of its limited hangout the pattern recognition abilities of investigators and journalists suddenly began to fail them.

Since the Hijackers of 9/11 fame were connected to the anthrax attacks, and since the anthrax attacks manifestly had to be planned and carried out by deep insiders in the U.S., there is no avoiding the implication that the 9/11 attacks were also carried out by insiders. There is, as it happens, a large body of research that supports this thesis.[5]

(d) The anthrax attacks were the result of a conspiracy meant to help redefine the enemy of the West, revising the global conflict framework from the Cold War to the Global War on Terror.

The Introduction set out my understanding of "conspiracy" and the point has by now been made repeatedly that the anthrax attacks—obviously criminal and secretly planned—were the acts of a group. I have also explained why no hypothesis of an opportunist loner or an opportunistic group is adequate. Flexibility, the seizing of opportunities, the ability to move quickly from option A to option B: all these can be found, but they took place within the context of a plan.

The shift from the Cold War to the Global War on Terror has been discussed mainly through the case of U.S. withdrawal from the ABM treaty. Narrowly, terrorism, together with its frequent partner the rogue state with WMD, was to be the new enemy. The immediate exemplars of these enemies were meant to be the shadowy and ubiquitous al-Qaeda and its state sponsors, Afghanistan, the home of the 9/11 planners, and Iraq, the home of the WMD used in the anthrax attacks. Broadly, the enemy was now Islam—officially "extremist" Islam, but, through contagion, all of Islam.

(e) The establishment of the Global War on Terror, to which the anthrax attacks contributed, enabled the U.S. executive branch to reduce the civil liberties of people in the U.S. and to attack other nations. Domestically and externally, these events were also used to weaken the rule of law.

Chapter 3 showed that the anthrax attacks, and repeated threats of attacks, were used to move the Patriot Act through Congress.

The perpetrators' approach to domestic law can be seen both in the intimidation of the legislative branch, as in the case of the Patriot Act, and in the marginalizing of both legislative and judicial branches, as in the setting up of military tribunals for trying suspects within the framework of the Global War on Terror.

A host of other initiatives not discussed in this book also have depended on the argument that the United States is at war and that, therefore, the executive needs increased powers. This argument carries less weight at the international level, of course, and U.S. leaders have had to exert a great deal of effort to bring the international community with them on their adventures. Aware of this, and convinced the benefits of imperial might outweigh those of international citizenship, the executive has followed the PNAC plan of either disengaging from international agreements or simply violating them.

***

What is to be said about the success or failure of the anthrax operation? The attacks were certainly successful in causing an infusion of funds into bioweapons work in the U.S. Already in 2008, *Scientific American* noted that the 2001 attacks "sparked a massive infusion of research funds to counter civilian bioterrorism, $41 billion spread over seven federal departments and agencies."[6] By 2011 the 2002-2011 expenditures were estimated at $70 billion.[7]

In 2008 a large new biodefense laboratory, to cost $143 million and occupy 160,000 square feet, was dedicated at Fort Detrick, Maryland. This is where the late Bruce Ivins, driven to his death by the FBI, had worked. When it opened, Jamie Johnson, of the Department of Homeland Security, said: "This is a great day."[8]

But if those institutions that grow fat on military spending were made happy by the anthrax attacks, the failures of the operation are also noteworthy. The attempt to implicate Muslim groups and states collapsed almost immediately after the Patriot Act was pushed through Congress. The decision to invade Iraq, made well before 9/11, was not changed but its justification now depended on a set of unvarnished lies that failed to convince the international community. U.S. leaders had no Security Council cover and, therefore, no legal justification whatsoever for their clear act of aggression. This was not a trivial failure. While it demonstrated the unilateralism that groups such as the Project for the New American Century championed, ignoring international law had a price. The price was erosion of international sympathy for the U.S. government and a growing conviction that the U.S. was itself a rogue state run by criminals.

Endnotes

1 Michael Isikoff and David Corn, *Hubris: The Inside Story of Spin, Scandal, and the Selling of the Iraq War* (New York: Three Rivers Press, 2006).

2 Kevin Ryan, *Another Nineteen: Investigating Legitimate 9/11 Suspects* (U.S.A.: Microbloom, 2013).

3 "Limited Hangout," *Wikipedia*, n.d., https://en.wikipedia.org/wiki/Limited_hangout.

4 Ibid.

5 All of David Ray Griffin's books on 9/11 are good, and the following set is an excellent place to start: Griffin, *The New Pearl Harbor: Disturbing Questions about the Bush Administration and 9/11 (updated Edition)*; Griffin, *The New Pearl Harbor Revisited: 9/11, the Cover-Up, and the Exposé*. Special mention should also be made of *The 9/11 Toronto Report: International Hearings on the Events of September 11, 2001* (Dallas, Texas: International Center for 9/11 Studies, 2013). Also helpful is philosopher John McMurtry's "The Moral Decoding of 9-11: Beyond the U.S. Criminal State," *Journal of 9/11 Studies* 35 (February 2013): 1–67. Websites that provide a solid critical perspective on 9/11 include:

 9/11 Consensus Panel:
 http://www.consensus911.org/
 Journal of 9/11 Studies:
 http://www.journalof911studies.com/
 Architects & Engineers for 9/11 Truth:
 http://www.ae911truth.org/

6 John Miller, "Postal Anthrax Aftermath: Has Biodefense Spending Made Us Safer?" *Scientific American*, November 6, 2008.

7 Leitenberg, "Biological Weapons: Where Have We Come from over the Past 100 Years?" I disagree with Leitenberg on important aspects of both the 9/11 and the anthrax attacks, but his point about the emptiness of bioweapons warnings is well made.

8 Nelson Hernandez, "Huge New Biodefense Lab Is Dedicated at Fort Detrick," *Washington Post*, October 23, 2008.

APPENDIX

THE SEPTEMBER 20 ST. PETERSBURG LETTER

Was the September 20, 2001 letter sent from St. Petersburg, Florida to Tom Brokaw of NBC News a component of the anthrax attacks? Or was the mailing a separate occurrence that had no relation to the anthrax attacks? The issue is important for several reasons, one of which is that it was this St. Petersburg letter that began its message with "THE UNTHINKABEL."

Most researchers have followed the FBI's lead, concluding that the St. Petersburg letter was a separate and unrelated phenomenon. However, Barbara Rosenberg, a leading critic of the FBI's investigation and one of the authors of the *Bioterrorism & Biodefense* articles referred to in Chapter 5, suggested as early as 2002 that the set of St. Petersburg letters, to which the letter to Brokaw belonged, should be taken seriously as possible components of the anthrax operation.[1] Researcher Ed Lake responded that the St. Petersburg letters were not linked to the anthrax letter attacks and were irrelevant to the study of the anthrax attacks.[2]

A review of Lake's arguments will show the weakness of his position.

(1) Lake said it made no sense that people possessing real anthrax should send hoax letters. They might send threat letters, he said, but not hoax letters. "The psychology," he claimed, "is all wrong." But even if he was right about "the psychology" (he provided no evidence to support this claim), everything we know about the St. Petersburg letter sent to Brokaw suggests it actually was a threat letter, not a hoax letter. That is, it did not pretend to contain anthrax spores. According to those who saw this letter, it contained phrases such as "see what happens next" and "sample of how it will look."[3] In other words, the letter was *threatening* actual attacks.

Is it credible that such threats might be part of a bioterrorism attack? Certainly, it is—as Lake admitted. The Dark Winter simulation of June, 2001 included, alongside dissemination of actual biological agents, threat letters sent to news media.

(2) Lake referred to the numerous hoax and threat letters that are regularly sent through the U.S. mail ("the Postal Service investigated more than 80 threats involving anthrax every year"), arguing that the St. Petersburg letters were mailed by "nut cases" and were unrelated to the actual 2001 attacks. While it is true that coincidence cannot be ruled out, Lake proceeded much too quickly to his coincidence theory. He did not give due weight to the coincidences that would have been required.

Both the St. Petersburg threat letter and a potentially lethal spore-laden letter from New Jersey were sent to the same person at the same news media office in the same city (Tom Brokaw at NBC TV in New York City).). They were sent at nearly the same time: the threat letter postmarked September 20, the anthrax letter postmarked September 18. Moreover, although the writing on the two envelopes suggests different authors, the similarities in style are noteworthy: the addresses in both cases have been hand-printed in capital letters with four lines of text giving information in the same sequence with minimal punctuation.[4]

(3) Lake's final argument had to do with the copycat phenomenon. Copycat criminals, he said, will send hoax or threat letters after a genuine article is made public. He implied that the St. Petersburg letters can be dismissed for this reason. But neither the deadly anthrax letter postmarked on September 18 nor any of the other anthrax letters in the attacks was known to the public when the September 20 threat letter was sent. The writer of the September 20 letter, if he or she was an ordinary member of the public, could not have been "copying" any of the letters sent in the anthrax attacks.

It is true that already by September 20, 2001 fear of imminent anthrax attacks had been expressed in the news media, as indicated in Chapter 6, but there was little public discussion at this time about the sending of anthrax spores to media persons via letters (the Dark Winter exercise, for example, was not well known at this time). Dispersion of an agent through letters as a method of biological warfare is quite different from dispersion through the much-feared and much-discussed crop-dusters.

Quite apart from Ed Lake's arguments, it is important to remember that the September 20 threat letter was part of a set of three. Don Foster, the university professor given access by the FBI to the letters, has pointed to the "same backward N's and Russian quotes" used in the letters—surely not coincidental similarities.[5] We can, therefore, say that whoever sent this set of letters established, via the repeated St. Petersburg postmarks, a Florida connection of the sort that would later become a vital feature of the actual anthrax attacks. Moreover, the person or persons who sent this set of letters also drew a connection to Judith Miller (one of the three St. Petersburg letters went to her address at *The New York Times*), and Miller was a key player over several years in the campaign to frighten the U.S. public with stories about Russia and Iraq as bioterrorism threats. Miller's St. Petersburg letter allowed her to claim victimhood and helped make the book, *Germs*, published in early October of 2001, a bestseller.

For the above reasons, I regard it as very likely that the September 20 St. Petersburg letter was a component of the anthrax operation.

Endnotes

1 Ed Lake, "Hoaxes, Psychology & Barbara Hatch Rosenberg," *The Anthrax Attacks*, July 6, 2003, http://www.anthraxinvestigation.com/HoaxVs-Real.html.

2 Ibid.

3 "Anxious About Anthrax: A Few Cases Do Not an Epidemic Make.," *Newsweek*, October 22, 2001; Don Foster, "The Message in the Anthrax," *Vanity Fair, as Reproduced at: http://www.ph.ucla.edu/epi/Bioter/messageanthrax.html*, October 2003.

4 See:http://www.fbi.gov/about-us/history/famous-cases/anthrax-amerithrax/the-envelopes-2; http://members.tripod.com/anthrax_hoaxes/ANTHRAX_HOAXES/INDEX.HTML

5 Foster, "The Message in the Anthrax."

INDEX

Made in the USA
Las Vegas, NV
01 December 2023

81938150R00118